AHEAD
OF THE
GAME

AHEAD
OF THE
GAME

JAMES COPPINGER

FOREWORD BY SIR KENNY DALGLISH

DB
PUBLISHING

First published 2021 by DB Publishing, an imprint of JMD Media Ltd,
Nottingham, United Kingdom.

Written with John Carter

ISBN 9781780916248

Printed in the UK by TJ Books Ltd

CONTENTS

FOREWORD

I WAS THE manager of Newcastle United in 1998 when we bought James and another boy, Paul Robinson, from Darlington. We didn't have a reserve team at the club and were trying to build one up because we thought it was important for the younger element to have something to aspire to after they had finished in the youth team.

James was a decent young player. I watched some of his early games and he did well, but at 17 it was a big ask to move clubs from Darlington to Newcastle even though it was just up the road. He looked to be a good prospect at the time and I'm pleased that he's had such a long and impressive career. To play for 24 years and in 800 games, up until the age of 40 – with 16 years and more than 600 games at one club – shows his professionalism and loyalty. He's not done too badly.

I agree with the philosophy that James promotes in this book: having the right mindset and attitude doesn't do you any harm at all. It must be of benefit. If you've got a bad attitude you're not going to do as well as you would hope or be capable of doing. It can't be any other way.

People point towards the need to handle disappointments when they come along, but you've also got to be able to handle the good things. It's very easy when things are going well to think you're complete. You're never complete. When you have success it's fantastic but it brings its challenges and it's important to handle it correctly. You don't want to throw it away.

I was fortunate, I played for Celtic and Liverpool who were two of the most successful clubs of their time and the players there were mentally strong. If you've got a good attitude and you're in the right place at the right time then you'll get success. I'd add that everybody also needs a bit of good fortune at some stage of your career, and having ability never does you any harm. I think those principles apply in football, other sports and every walk of life.

Clubs, managers and other specialists can help players but, ultimately, attitude comes from within yourself. You've got to be aware and strong enough to know what you're doing wrong and try to put it right. If you're playing for a football club and a manager they want you to be every bit as successful as you want to be yourself, so work with them.

I wish James every luck with this book and hope the readers – and particularly aspiring young footballers – will enjoy reading about his career and how he developed such a professional mind-set.

THE INVISIBLE FOUNDATION

1

THOUSANDS OF YOUNGSTERS dream of making it to football's Premier League, arguably the best and most competitive league on the planet. But I wasn't one of them. In fact, I never wanted to be a professional footballer.

Yet, on Saturday 26 August 2000, at the age of 19 years and seven months, I found myself standing by the side of the pitch at Newcastle United's St James' Park, the eyes of 51,573 spectators on me, about to make my debut for the club.

'Don't let me down, son.'
Instructions from Sir Bobby Robson before making my Premier League debut.
© Newcastle United Football Club

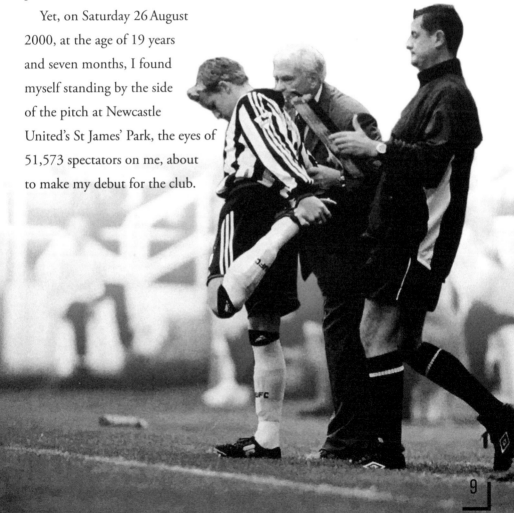

Next to me was the legendary manager Sir Bobby Robson, who issued last-minute tactical instructions then kissed his hand, patted my face and said 'don't let me down, son,' which was a kind of good luck gesture, albeit a strange one! With that I was on, a 79th-minute substitute, partnering the Geordie icon Alan Shearer upfront.

For most supporters those remaining 11 minutes and injury time were uneventful and forgettable as we held onto our 2-0 advantage over Tottenham Hotspur. For me, though, the memories still give me goosebumps, 20 years later. It seemed like the start of something special. By then Sir Bobby had likened my playing style to the Italy and Chelsea superstar Gianfranco Zola and to have progressed to this elite level at such an early age was quite an achievement, particularly as I'd been playing amateur Sunday League football just a couple of years previously! I thought I'd

On the ball against Tottenham. In truth, at 19 years of age, I wasn't mentally or physically ready to shine at this elite level.

© Newcastle United Football Club

made it, but how wrong I was! Because, in hindsight, that brief taste of the Premier League was as much of an end as a beginning. It was the only first-team game I played at Newcastle and at that standard.

I just wasn't ready to shine on the pitch with the quality of footballers that graced St James' that day: Shearer, Gary Speed, Sol Campbell and Darren Anderton to name a few.

In fact, that peak was followed by some serious dips, and during some troubled early stages of my career it looked like I might become a sporting case of 'what-might-have-been'. Thankfully, with expert help, I became aware of what I was missing, tackled my problems, rebuilt my career and kicked on to rack up 800 professional games in a career that spanned 24 years, playing until I was 40 years old. As Sir Kenny Dalglish wrote in his foreword, in the end I didn't do too badly. *Ahead of the Game* is about my rollercoaster story and, in particular, the invisible but most essential attribute for every footballer. Without doubt my growing capability in this area was the primary reason for my success.

▌MAIN ATTRIBUTES

So, let's start with my take on the main attributes that I believe are needed to play at the highest level.

The first is **technique**. This involves heading, passing, shooting dribbling, tackling and the like. A youngster can develop beyond the foundation skills and move up levels; to the next one, the next one and the next one. There's no limit, at least until they reach

Messi's incredible standard! Becoming able to control and master the football is critical.

The second attribute is **tactical awareness**, the ability to 'read' the game, adapt to different formations, and understand where you should be – dependent on the position you've been asked to play – both in and out of possession. Linked to this is the spatial awareness to have a 'picture' of what's going on around you, helping you to make good decisions. Nowadays, tactical awareness is essential, especially at the top level.

By the way, I'm inclined to agree with the view taken in Matthew Syed's well-known book *Bounce: How Champions are made* that states that the major factor in the development of the technical and tactical skills that I've just described is simply the number of hours of 'purposeful practice'. Over time and with repetition, a player may acquire skills that look effortless. They may even get misleadingly described as 'naturally talented'. To me that's a myth. You don't get born with it. There are no short cuts. You have to put in the hours.

I'd add, though, that I don't think the 'purposeful practice' *has* to be within a club, academy or centre of excellence, particularly in the formative years. No, I think back to what I know of my childhood heroes – the likes of Paul Gascoigne and the Brazilian Juninho – and when they were really young they just played, in playgrounds, streets and parks. That's all they ever did; a ball at their feet, having fun.

More recently Zlatan Ibrahimović was raised in the Rosengard district of Malmo, Sweden, where he played a brand of streetball on a makeshift pitch with friends; Sadio Mane played with other kids in abject poverty in Senegal; and Luis Suarez played shoeless football in the streets of Salto, Uruguay. Minimal facilities, not a coach in sight, but all developed an eye-catching individuality that was enhanced as they subsequently became sucked into the system and associated with clubs.

So that's two of the main attributes – technique and tactical awareness – covered. The third is **physical,** including strength, speed, agility and fitness. There are some traits, such as height and, to some extent, speed, that are genetic but most can be developed with a dedicated approach to gym work and training.

▌INVISIBLE AND OVERLOOKED

Doubtless those three attributes – technical, tactical and physical – are all essential, but what gets the best out of them and brings them to life is the fourth, final and most important attribute: mental performance.

In my opinion a professional mindset is the key that unlocks everything else. If a footballer is confident, resilient, works hard, possesses self-belief and leadership skills and acts professionally then they will operate from a foundation that supports the technical, tactical and physical skills and will allow them to make the most of what they've got.

Just how important is mastering the mental game? Of course, it's impossible to accurately assign a specific percentage as each player approaches game preparation and performance in his or her unique way. Yet most agree that a big part of football is mental and when I ask them to give me a percentage, their answers are always over 50 per cent and sometimes as high as 90 per cent. Certainly, I know that players who develop their mental performance dramatically increase their chances of success.

However, because that all occurs in the footballer's brain it's often overlooked in coaching, up to and including professional level. Coaches can *see* a player control a ball or watch someone sweat in the gym and *see* how they become bigger or stronger, but they can't *see* how a player is thinking. Of course, there are usually some indications there if the coach looks hard enough but it's less obvious and many struggle with that.

Equally, if a player wants to improve their shooting or heading then they can go out and practice on the training pitch and, over time, the improvement is obvious. If they want to develop their upper body strength they can go into the gym and become able to lift more weights. But how do you improve mental performance – and how do you measure it? That's why I feel coaches and players don't understand it and, often, don't want to understand it. It scares people because they can't see it. Plus, even in the 21st century, there's still stigma within football in focusing on the mind. As a result most concentrate elsewhere.

▮ HIGH ACHIEVERS ...

During my career I've observed some pros, like Alan Shearer, my teammate at Newcastle, who had the lot: incredible technique (particularly as a goalscorer), tactical awareness, quick and strong as an ox, mentally as tough and resilient as they come. Like all the elite players Shearer had deep reserves of self-belief and ambition and, no doubt, he powered through to the top, always moving his game onto the next level, and the next level and the next level.

More recently Harry Kane stands out. I've spoken to someone who coached him at Tottenham and he told me that at the age of 13 Harry didn't stand out. But as he got to 14, 15 and 16 he developed mentally and decided he was going to dedicate himself to the game and work hard to improve. His mindset became incredibly professional from then on and he soon overtook the youngsters at Spurs who had been ahead of him. If you listen to Harry speak now he talks about loan spells where it didn't work out. Yet he used those experiences to make himself a better player. What an incredible footballer and role model he's become; never satisfied, always trying toimprove.

Shearer and Kane: two magnificent sportsmen with the all-round package to make it at the very top of their profession and stay there for many years.

It isn't just international superstars who have impressed me, though. There are pros in the English Football League that have sustained some good careers through a strong mentality. I'm an admirer of Adebayo

'There are footballers who are very good playing on the outside but don't know what to do inside.

Then there are players who are very good inside but don't have the physique, the legs, to go outside.'

Pep Guardiola

Akinfenwa at Wycombe Wanderers. He talks about 'beast mode' mentality. That's his thing, it works for him and he consistently delivers. He played in the Championship for the first time at 38 years old. He does things differently to me, but he's found a way that suits him.

■ ... AND UNDER-ACHIEVERS

However, I've played with hundreds of teammates that didn't achieve all they could have done simply because they never developed the right mindset.

I saw it in their body language, their negative self-talk and the way they dealt with disappointment.

Doubtless, some might have been influenced by their upbringing, their surroundings and the people they spent most of their time with. Whatever the reasons, I saw under-performers at every level: Non-League, League Two, League One, the Championship, even the Premier League – and the sad thing is that most of them weren't even aware of it. They probably knew that something was missing but had no idea what it was. Or maybe they just weren't willing and self-disciplined enough to take action. I get that it's not easy to remove yourself from a friendship group even if you know it's a problem. It's not easy to sacrifice things. It's not easy to be consistent with your habits and behaviours. So not everyone has the daily discipline to do what they know, deep down, is required of them.

Certainly, you need mental strength to cope with the scrutiny that you get from managers, coaches, the media (including social media) and supporters in modern-day football. There's so much expected from you. You're in a high-pressure industry that demands results and performances and you have to deliver. People judge you each time you play and they don't take into account what's happening in your personal life and your headspace. How could they? That's the ruthlessness of professional sport.

That's why I feel like it's so important to think the right way. So why not take control of it? Why not try to understand how to improve it? It's not something to be scared of. It's a must if you want to be successful because your mind dictates whether you fulfil your potential. Certainly, the players that become aware of the potential to improve and get help (some came to me for advice) are much more likely to work it out and put it right.

▋LIFELINE

Part of my ability to spot flaws in mindset is because in the early part of my career – when I made that Premier League debut at St James Park for instance – I struggled in this area. So my early success didn't last very long.

To be fair, I had a reasonable attitude in my youth, albeit without consciously working on it. Without the appetite for 'purposeful practice' as Matthew Syed described it, I wouldn't have improved my technique and tactical skills so quickly. Yet I got to the age of 23 years with zero self-awareness of my mental performance. As a result, I wasn't translating my training ground form onto the pitch on a match-day. Fortunately, my manager at Doncaster Rovers, Dave Penney, introduced me to someone who opened my eyes. It was a real light-bulb moment, almost spiritual, like an awakening. We had life-changing conversations that helped me transform not only my football career but my whole life. He was the mentor, the lifeline, that I needed and since then I've spent 17 years trying to put it all into practice. It was the single most important reason why I played professionally until the age of 40.

People who spoke to me before that pivotal moment in my career wouldn't believe that I'm the same person now! I've changed so much in my mental approach and it enhanced my performance and results massively. Football is a mind game and success starts in the head. In 24 years as a professional that's the biggest thing I learned.

▌HIT BY A METEORITE!

Now I talk about it all the time, working with youngsters who want a career in football, helping them understand how important it is to master the mental game and explaining what they can do to improve. I'm also trying to break down the stigma. Developing in this area isn't a sign of weakness or evidence that there's a problem that needs to be solved. It's simply about using the power of the mind to get the best out of technical, tactical and physical attributes.

I know that without the whole package of attributes the odds are stacked against them. I know that statistics suggest that of the children who enter academies at the age of nine, less than one per cent will make it to become one of around 4,000 registered members of English Professional Footballers Association (PFA). And I know that just 180 children of the 1.5 million who play organised youth football at any one time will become one of around 500 PFA registered players within the Premier League. That's just 0.012 per cent; about the same chance as being hit by a meteorite!

Simply put, if a footballer sustains a career in League One or Two it places them in an exclusive group. It's a massive achievement. To climb even further up the football pyramid to the Premier League means they are truly elite, the best of the best.

I don't share those numbers to be a kill-joy or dampen ambition but simply to highlight that with the standards so astronomically high an aspiring footballer's chances will be massively multiplied if they possess a professional's mindset. Nowadays, it isn't optional. It's essential.

And that's why I've written this book, breaking the subject down into seven sections, reflecting different phases of my career:

Love and Inspiration
Self-belief and Confidence
Resilience and Courage
Self-awareness and Accountability
Teamwork and Consistency
Leadership and Communication
Professionalism

Then, within each section, there are three main areas:

My story. This element is crucial because I'm certain aspiring footballers will be able to relate to the challenges I faced along the way and the mistakes I made which helped me to improve my mental performance. My story should help to place my guidance in context and bring it to life.

Eyewitness contributions – independently gathered – from some people who have been closely involved in my career.

And finally, **analysis, reflections and takeaways**.

Maybe if the 19-year-old James Coppinger who made that brief Premier League debut against Spurs all those years ago had read and acted upon a book like

© Newcastle United Football Club

this then the first part of his career would have been less of a rollercoaster and he would have been even better equipped to make the most of the opportunity that presented itself!

All ifs, buts and maybes in my case – and it would be churlish to have any regrets after an 800 game, 24-year pro career – but now I'm keen that my words and guidance help others to appreciate the importance of a professional mindset at an early stage so that they can get ahead of the game and develop the skills to maximise their potential.

Opposite and previous: Either end of my career. I was always decent technically and tactically and I didn't change too much either physically – but in terms of the 'invisible foundation' of mindset there is no comparison between these two versions of me.

LOVE AND INSPIRATION

2

MIND-MAPS

FROM NOW ON mindset is the theme that runs through this book and my long footballing story. We are all a product of our childhood and my early mindset was highly influenced by my parents, my wider family, my friends, the place where we lived, events and the media. We can add into the mix my personality and genetic make-up.

This cocktail of influences led to habits and patterns of thinking that were unique to me, creating what I call a 'mind-map'. We're all wired differently so each person's mind map is different, like a fingerprint – but where it differs from a fingerprint is that it has the potential to change and develop.

So, what influences and events in my childhood years shaped my mindset?

▌BUBBLE

I grew up in Guisborough, a small town near Middlesbrough in the North East of England, with a tight-knit family living around me in a kind of bubble that included my mum, dad, sister, aunties and uncles, nanas and grandads.

A happy family in our Guisborough bubble. Mam (Maureen), Dad (John), Sister (Alix) and me.
© James Coppinger

I would say that the most influential people in my life were my mum, dad, sister Alix and my nana and grandad (known to me as 'Granda Herbert' because he was my mum's dad). I thought mum was very strict when I was a kid. She was a cub leader. We were always going somewhere, we always had to be organised, and we always had to be on time, if not ten minutes early. She was a constant worrier just like my nana, my mum's mum. Dad worked for BT, loved football and played as an amateur. He sacrificed a lot for me and went to nearly all my games, including sleeping in the car a few times because he hadn't got time to get home after the match. One of my first memories was my dad putting on a video cassette of a game of football. It was end-to-end action and I remember watching and thinking 'this is unbelievable'!

Grandad also loved football with almost childlike enthusiasm. He'd take me to games when Mum or

Dad couldn't and I always felt comfortable and happy around him. He was jovial; always laughing, always joking, always believing in me.

So perhaps it was natural that I began to get into football. I was never forced to do anything by my parents, but I grew up in the 1990s where I could be out and about in the evening, playing football on the grass outside my house or down the park with three, four or five good friends until the fading light at 9 or 10pm in the summer. Even in the cold of a North-East winter, we'd be out.

Early days but already loving football. Here with Mark Robinson, who has become a lifelong friend.
© James Coppinger

Sometimes we'd go to someone's house and watch a video of '100 Great Goals' and then go to the park to try and replicate them. We also went to the park after I got new goalkeeper gloves. Taking it in turns we'd get over one side of the goal. Someone would curl a shot towards the top corner and we'd dive across trying to tip it round the post. And I remember getting the Dutch National school team shirt and brand new Predator boots that had just come out for Christmas. As soon as they were unwrapped I was bursting to get out, play football and pretend I was one of my idols. Every time I think about those happy, fun-free times I feel nostalgic.

Nor was it just football. In the summer we used to play a lot of cricket and tennis as well. I learned a lot from playing different sports, but football was always number one.

I played in the team at my Primary School, Belmont Junior School between the age of seven and ten, and we got through three or four rounds of a nationwide Smith's Crisps football competition. One more win and we would have gone to Wembley and taken penalties at half-time in front of a massive crowd while there was an England game going on. Unfortunately, we just missed out but that experience was magical. We had a hell of a team and subsequently the school has never gone on to better that record.

▌NESSUM DORMA

It was around that time that the 1990 World Cup took place in Italy. That was another inspiration. Gazza and England made it through to the semi-finals under

Bobby Robson's (he was knighted and became Sir Bobby in 2002) management. I still have the kit and can still remember the team 30 years later – players like David Platt, Chris Waddle, Stuart Pearce, Paul Gascoigne and Gary Lineker. Gazza got booked in the semi-final and I remember crying, wanting Germany to win because I knew that he wouldn't be able to play in the final. I can almost go back to the nine-year-old me and that feeling of disappointment and frustration and anger. That's testament to how much it influenced me.

And it wasn't just England. There were many other memorable moments at that World Cup: Toto Schillaci scoring goal after goal, the little green, red and white Italian stick mascot and Pavarotti's famous operatic song *Nessum Dorma*. Every time I hear it it takes me back to that amazing, magical tournament. Brilliant memories.

By then in addition to my school team, I was playing on Sundays for the Teesside-based, Marton Juniors. I started there when I was seven or eight years of age and went right through to the under 15s. The club was renowned for bringing players through like Jonathan Woodgate, Stewart Downing and Graeme Lee and we had a brilliant team. We won the league every season.

▌FOOTBALL MAD

Without knowing it I was developing technical, tactical and physical skills that defined the kind of footballer I became.

I was always good technically. I had a football everywhere I went as a kid and was always playing with my mates at the park or for schools or clubs. So I put in a lot of 'purposeful practice' learning the game. My ability to control the ball as well as more advanced skills like applying different curve and spin on a shot, picking a pass, turning out of trouble, dropping my shoulder to unbalance opponents and dribble past them all came from that grounding.

I also became tactically aware. I watched football on TV avidly with my dad, had a season ticket at Middlesbrough for a while and supported Nottingham Forest – all the while soaking in information about how to play the game and aspiring to copy my heroes. Although I wasn't the most academic pupil at school I was a keen student of football. In fact, I was football mad and always attentive when my managers and coaches talked about tactics; a trait that helped me to contribute to teams from different positions.

And I became extremely fit because I was so active. I felt like I could run and run and run and that core fitness never left me. However, I was unusually little and lightweight. I wasn't as tall or strong as many of my teammates or opponents, and I had to adapt my game to make use of my strengths.

As for the fourth and most important attribute: mental performance? Well, at this stage I was oblivious to what that even meant!

■ 'HAT-TRICK TODAY, JIMBO!'

During my time at Belmont and, particularly, Marton my mum, dad and grandads were usually there. Mum used to scream and shout encouragement on the side-lines, lost in the excitement of the game (when I turned professional she stopped coming as she found it so stressful). Dad was a constant presence, albeit quieter, and both my grandads videoed each game.

Grandad Herbert was a one-off. I now owned 'Quasar Lineker' boots and he took them to his garage and cleaned them after every game. Then, before the next game, he would regularly put motivational notes on the bottom of the boots with masking tape – something like 'hat-trick today Jimbo!' and 'let's get a goal'. When I took them into the changing rooms the lads used to laugh and joke about it but I didn't care.

At Marton there were three or four from Middlesbrough that got on the ball, dribbled past everybody and racked up the goals. I let them have the limelight, setting them up and assisting. I was a team player, trying to gel everybody together. I remember that when I got Player of the Year at under-13 or under-14 level that was why the coaches said I was chosen. I understood the good players, the ones who

The renowned Marton Juniors! On the far left in the front row, left to right, are Greg Booth, me and Mark Robinson.

© James Coppinger

were on the same wavelength as me, and made that work on the pitch.

Maybe that was an early sign of a few character traits: a small-town mentality and unselfishness. I was, though, also opinionated and strong-willed. As I moved into my teenage years if I didn't want to do something I didn't do it. For instance, with cross country at school if I fancied it I'd win. If I didn't I'd finish last. I think my parents struggled with that. Teachers saw the ability in me, but they couldn't get it out. It frustrated them to see that I could do whatever I wanted to but couldn't always get motivated.

I always believed I was as good as anyone else on the football pitch, but if I walked into a room I would never be that person who stood up in front of everybody and was confident enough to take control of the situation. In fact, my confidence reduced during my teenage years. I wouldn't say I was bullied at school but I was sensitive to criticism. If people had a go at me I struggled to deal with it and let it affect me.

So I remember now that at Laurence Jackson Secondary School two teachers didn't believe in me. One managed both our school and the county football team – and left me out of the county team for a lad in my position from another school who was a 5ft 10in battering ram who could barge people out of the way.

Some coaches just want players who can help them win games at that moment. It's so short-sighted and it's become a bugbear of mine. It still goes on in the modern game. Harry Kane was released from Arsenal's academy because of a lack of height and pace and

Marcus Rashford was on Manchester City's radar as a nine-year-old but was judged to be too small and they didn't pick him up.

Ironically, the teacher at my school was a Newcastle fan, and when I got signed by them he asked for tickets for games from me. However much I might have been tempted, I did arrange the tickets and didn't hold a grudge!

ON TRIAL

My best friends when I was growing up were Greg Booth, my cousin, and Mark Robinson. They played at Marton Juniors with me and were both excellent footballers, dead set on becoming a professional. Greg's dad (my uncle) was the opposite of my placid and laid-back dad. He was relentless; pushing him, and pushing him and pushing him. I remember sitting in the back of their car once on the way home from a game and I was almost in tears because of the way his dad was talking to him. I was thinking 'Greg played really well today' and his dad is having a go. My dad wouldn't ever say anything when I got in the car after a game, but Greg's would grill him. Chalk and cheese.

Greg and Mark took football seriously; I didn't. They had clarity, drive and ambition; I just lived (quite happily) from day to day, taking each one as it came. They were my best friends but I just wasn't like them. I didn't *see* myself as a professional footballer. To be honest I didn't *see* what my future might involve at all. I just enjoyed playing with my mates, riding my bike and being a kid.

Why was I like that? It's difficult to self-analyse more than 20 years later, but whilst on the surface I could be opinionated and stubborn, deep down I think I lacked confidence, feared failure and didn't like the idea of being taken out of what I knew. If I didn't aim high and put myself forward then I couldn't be rejected or embarrassed or criticised.

‘YOU NEVER LOOK BOTHERED, YOU NEVER LOOK INTERESTED’

Perhaps the previous chapters in this book highlighted some reasons for that mindset: the close-knit community in a small town, the encouraging but laid-back family around me, the small physique. Whatever the reason it never entered my head to become a professional footballer.

In some ways that doesn't make sense. If I loved playing football so much and could play the game so well then why wouldn't I consider turning pro when many of my friends were trying to go down that route? And, as if that isn't confusing enough, then if it hadn't occurred to me to become a pro then why did I go for several trials? I suppose it was just the scrambled thoughts of a mixed-up teenager's brain.

Because I was part of the best team in the league in our area the opportunity was always there to have trials and I tagged along with my mates to the big three in the local area – Middlesbrough, Newcastle and Sunderland – as well as the team I supported, Nottingham Forest.

I went to the Middlesbrough Centre of Excellence when it was upstairs at Ayresome Park's indoor facility. I didn't enjoy it, though. We were taught Cruyff turns, stepovers and the like – but it felt quite regimented and straight out of the coaching manual. I got told I was okay to come along and train but was too small to play much in the games.

I did get selected to play as a substitute against Blackpool, though, in a match I vividly remember even though I didn't kick a ball. I stood on the side-lines the whole game, never got on and said, 'Dad, look, this isn't for me. I'm not coming all this way and not playing.'

So he went and spoke to one of the Middlesbrough coaches and said, 'Look, our James doesn't want to do this.' The coach was surprised: 'What do you mean?' 'Well, he doesn't want to stand on the side and not be involved.' The coach said, 'There are people who would give their right arm to do this,' and my dad responded, 'Well, it isn't what James wants to do, so we're not going to keep him here.'

My relationship with Middlesbrough was a bit love-hate. I had a season ticket there for a while to watch Bryan Robson's team with Emerson and Ravanelli and, in particular, Juninho, who was my idol and inspiration. I loved him. He was unreal and outrageous, someone who always had me on the edge of my seat and played with freedom unlike anything I'd seen before. I was 14 and wanted to be him basically because he was my type of player: slight, light and clever. But I resented Middlesbrough because they told me I was too small and didn't play me. That non-game at Blackpool has always annoyed me and in a way, it probably encouraged me to prove people wrong. That's another character trait I've always had; there have been several instances like that I've used as motivation. I enjoy doing that. Funnily enough, I ended up coming back to Middlesbrough with Newcastle for an FA Youth Cup tie and played well, scoring in a 5-1 win.

The trials continued. I went to Sunderland, stayed in some digs, did well but didn't fancy it, then had a trial for Nottingham Forest, the team I supported. I had all the kits, Stan Collymore was my favourite player and I admired the way they played football. I watched and looked up to players like Steve Stone, Ian Woan, Stuart Pearce and Mark Crossley. But when I stayed there overnight I rang my nana on the phone, almost in tears because I was so homesick. This was all a bit overwhelming and a big deal for me. I was part of a family that never really stepped out of their comfort zone.

I kind of believed in myself when I was on a football pitch but I never put myself forward. At these trials I always just blended into the background, letting the cocksure, confident, big-city boys hog the limelight. If you're a coach or a manager assessing players you will always gravitate to the ones who are giving off the best body language and are communicating; the ones who look like they've got a bit about them. That was never me. They would have never looked at me and thought 'he's desperate to be a pro footballer'. My dad always said, 'You never look bothered, you never looked interested.' That was true on the pitch and I also projected that image after getting rejected. I always said, 'I'm not arsed, I don't care,' which I think was all part of a kind of self-protection.

By the time I went for trials at Newcastle, Marton Juniors had folded at the under-15 level because a lot of our players had gone off to play for the likes of Manchester United, Middlesbrough and Sunderland in their Schools of Excellence. My best friends, Mark Robinson went to Nottingham Forest before doing a Youth Training Scheme (YTS) at Hartlepool, whilst Greg Booth became a YTS at Middlesbrough.

So I moved from Marton to Woodgarth to play with my mates. I loved it, got player of the year, was the top goalscorer, got noticed by Newcastle and was asked to train with them when I was 16 years old. I remember going up there in my Forest shirt, and they took the mickey out of me. I did well but there was a lad called Hoggy who told me, 'You've got no chance of getting in.' I think in the end only two – one of which was Shola Ameobi – got awarded a YTS or Scholarship and I wasn't one of them.

So, that was me done as far as Schools of Excellence were concerned. I'd had enough of being constantly told 'you can come and train with us' or 'you just need to grow a bit'. They saw my physique as a deal-breaker.

So I went back to Woodgarth and kept playing there purely as a hobby.

■ WHAT NEXT?

Would it have helped if I my parents had pushed me harder? Could my dad have provided the force and drive that I lacked? Perhaps if he had, it might have been different, but it wasn't in his nature and, besides,

I might have resented him and quit completely. I certainly don't think I'd have still been playing professional football when I was 40 years old. I took things personally. I don't know whether Greg resented his dad's well-meaning guidance at the time (I'm sure it was all done with the best of intentions) but I don't think he retained my love for the game.

Anyway, I went to a careers evening at Laurence Jackson, my secondary school, at the age of 16 with my mum and dad and walked through the kitchen area to all these stalls promoting various options, and they asked me 'what do you want to do?' I didn't have a clue. I went to a college taster day looking at architectural courses – and, subsequently, I went on to build my own house and project manage it – but I never once thought that was what I wanted to spend my life doing.

On reflection, I think there are lots of signposts in my childhood and development – some good, some bad – that explain the mind-map and mindset that I took into my adult life.

In truth, there was every chance that my life, post-school, was about to drift. Then everything changed. Up until now my life had been like the gentle part of a rollercoaster ride; slowly making an ascent to the highest point, with little change and few momentous events. Yet from the age of 16 to 23, in particular, my journey was about to be full of dizzying, disorientating twists and turns that tested me and my mindset to the max.

ANALYSIS

LOVE AND INSPIRATION

As I share my story in this book we will occasionally take a break from telling my story, pause for breath and analyse a quality that I believe is critical for pro footballers and helped me to play for so long.

One incredibly positive aspect of my childhood was that I fell in love with the game of football. I know that, along with self-belief, it became *the* most important part of my success and longevity in the game. Without it I wouldn't have been able to perform as a pro for more than 40 games every season for 18 years.

'I don't believe skill was, or ever will be, the result of coaches. It is a result of a love affair between the child and the ball.'

Roy Keane

▌ENJOYMENT

Funnily enough, I've found my enjoyment hasn't been particularly influenced by my age, the venue, who I played with or how many were watching. Whether it's playing in the park with my mates (nowadays it's more likely to be my kids); a mid-season, routine league game on a wet, cold Tuesday night; or playing at Wembley in front of 70,000 and a global audience on television, the feeling is much the same.

The same goes for training. I always looked forward to it. I never rolled out of bed and thought 'oh my God, I don't want to do this.'

Describing the feeling is difficult, of course, but it's a kind of love. There's a sensation inside your stomach that makes you feel alive. I got into an unconscious state, in the zone, totally absorbed in the game. I could have been anywhere.

There are so many aspects to the joy of football but competing, winning and achieving were all part of it. The

I love playing football: whether it's down the park with the kids, on the training ground or at a packed stadium, the feeling doesn't change.   © HeatherKingPhotography feeling when you're in the dressing room after a game, all shattered, and you've won and achieved something special is indescribable. Many retired players say that it's the team spirit, the camaraderie and the banter that they miss the most.

I also got real satisfaction out of training, where I conditioned myself to work hard and enjoy it. It was all about winning every day there as well. In five-a-sides I put everything into it, celebrating winning or scoring a goal as much as on a match-day! When I was training I wanted to do things properly. My view was 'why be half-arsed, why waste time being average, why waste time going through the motions?' Of course, I had days where I didn't feel quite 'up for it' or when things didn't go my way but they were important because if I could get through them, keep my head up and not drop my standards it built my strength and resilience. Then, if things went wrong on a match-day I could call upon that and manage it.

Academy players looked at me at training as if to say 'what is this guy doing?' but it was a habit. It's the feeling, it's the desire to perform well and to motivate and affect other people. Winning is always a buzz! I wasn't the best loser. I learned to deal with it and process it better later on. Deep down it still affected me, but I didn't let it show outwardly or affect my family life.

I've always been competitive in everything that I do, not just in sport but in life in general. I've just learned to tone it down. I want to be the best, I want to be the one everyone's talking about. I want to be *that* person. In football you have to be competitive because you're doing it every single day. You need drive and determination. There's always an opportunity to *not* perform, to *not* turn up, to get injured, to *not* fancy it. So having that love for football, in my opinion, helps you keep going and be successful for a longer period.

INSPIRING OTHERS

It would be great if you could bottle the love and enjoyment I've been writing about and sell it, but it's something that comes from within. You can't teach it or force it upon someone. However, I believe you *can* play a part in creating an environment that encourages and inspires others.

For me, inspiration was all around in my youth: my dad and Grandad Herbert with their almost naïve enthusiasm for the game; the friends who played with me in the park; the coaches at Marton and Woodgarth.

Add in the magic of the 1990 World Cup, and Nottingham Forest and Juninho, and, don't forget, above all, the out-of-body feeling of being absorbed in a match and the sense of success and achievement when it went well. I hope you can see why I fell for the game. I wasn't alone and football remains not only the most popular sport to watch in the United Kingdom, but also the most popular team sport to participate in, with 31 per cent of children aged between five and ten and 45 per cent of 11 to 15-year-olds playing football each month.

PRESSURE AND FEAR

By the way, I do think that too much structured coaching too early can begin to suck the enjoyment out of football. That's why I'm not the biggest fan of Academies. I've seen many youngsters become institutionalised. It becomes their be-all and end-all to beat the competition around them and 'make it' to become a pro. It's all they know, it can become all-consuming and I'm not sure that kind of obsessive behaviour is healthy, not least because they can become stale and tired of football.

I think Ajax in Holland have announced that they're not going to open Academies till the children are at least 11 or 12 years old. They will let the kids play within their teams and friends and just let them enjoy themselves, pressure-free, expectation-free before they take it too seriously.

Certainly, I've seen so many, of all ages, who have lost their way and fallen out of love with the game. As they grow older the biggest factor is pressure and fear. Fear comes in lots of guises: fear of failure, fear of not getting picked, fear of losing, fear of injury, and it always reduces enjoyment and performance levels.

'So many kids I see are tired of playing at 13 or 14 because they are training eight times a week. The pressure is full on. Kids need to be kids. They will grow and develop into the players they eventually will be.'

Ruud van Nistlerooy

That fear can be self-induced by negative thinking (much more on that later) and it can also come from external influences such as coaches and managers. They can have a huge influence, particularly on younger players who are more likely to get criticised. Some will be your best friend if you win and then throw teacups around and annihilate you if you lose. I don't think that works; it certainly didn't work for me. Don't get me wrong, if you play badly and lose then you shouldn't be happy – but nobody does that on purpose and I preferred managers who were consistent in focusing on performance rather than just results. In the modern game I think that, slowly, managers and coaches are a little bit more open to taking the time to analyse games before they start to dish the abuse out!

Nowadays that criticism is also dished out by fans, on social media as well as at the games. Pro footballers get scrutinised like never before and it affects some. Recently I worked with someone who's a fantastic player but got a little bit of stick because he's a team-player who sits in midfield and his contribution got overlooked. And it got to him. If you're 18, 19 and then all of a sudden the fans start criticising you, saying you're useless and you're this and that then it can be difficult.

When you're a pro there are so many distractions. When I was younger they got in the way massively. I felt that whenever I went out with people I had to pay and had to wear certain things and generally live up to the perception of a professional footballer. There's a lot of potential to lose your way, lose your sense of who you are and what you enjoy about playing, and the amount of money swilling about in modern football is a big part of that. It's had a massive impact on football and, in my opinion, it's only going to get worse. It would be a different game completely if everybody got paid the same. The way the world is, money creates power. Players think they are more powerful than they are and it's having a detrimental effect on their career.

Some who come through from bigger Academies can get paid far too much. By the time they get to 21, 22 years old they've never played a competitive game yet they have earned an absolute fortune. In my opinion, they may end up playing football for the wrong reasons; for the lifestyle rather than for the love of the game and to win things and be successful.

In the 2019/20 season Manchester City paid out an average £7 million in salaries to their playing squad. One of the many attractions of making it in the Premier League are those financial benefits, so it's not surprising that some get distracted by the pot of gold at the end of the rainbow or lose their mo-jo once they've experienced the lifestyle.

If it becomes all about the fame and the money that's a problem because they may not last. They might get to their 30s when the contracts become less lucrative and struggle because they've lost that love of the game.

▌SUPERPOWER

So an aspiring footballer needs to be aware of what can derail their career. Once the sense of why they started playing the game in the first place is lost and that childish, pure love of kicking a football around fades then motivation and performance will inevitably suffer.

Professionals who find that the very act of playing football still brings a smile to their face, remain free from cynicism and genuinely retain their passion are blessed with a superpower than will inspire their career and drive everything to the next level. It's that important!

> 'Success is no accident. It is hard work, perseverance, learning, studying, sacrifice and most of all, love of what you are doing or learning to do.'
>
> **Pelé**

TAKEAWAYS

■ Loving the game is a superpower that will help you to achieve excellence, success and longevity.

■ If you are open to it, inspiration can come in many forms including from people and events.

■ Fear, pressure and many other threats could lead to you falling out of love with the game. Be aware of them.

SELF-BELIEF AND CONFIDENCE

3

A PRAYER ANSWERED

RIGHT, BACK TO my story where, as a 16-year-old with no plans for the future it all looked bleak for me. Then I scored a hat-trick for Woodgarth against Darlington Spraire Lads in front of a watching Darlington scout. He approached my parents and asked if I wanted to go on trial. I did well and was called in to meet David Hodgson, their manager who offered me a two-year Youth Training Scheme (YTS) contract. The offer coincided with me leaving school so I decided to take them up on it, earning £42.50 a week. For me to be offered a YTS with Darlington, who were a League Two team at the time, was an honour.

▌LONG DAYS

It allowed me to spend time with my best friends, Greg and Mark, again. By now Greg was on the books at Middlesbrough and Mark was at Hartlepool, having been released by Nottingham Forest. So each morning we'd all get on the bus from Guisborough to Middlesbrough before heading off in our different directions. Greg would stay in Boro, Mark would get a connecting train to Hartlepool and I'd get one to Darlington Station before walking to their training ground at Feethams. Then we'd do it all in reverse on the way back. They were long days: six in the morning until six at night.

Being at Darlington was good for me. We had to work hard, cleaning and painting the changing rooms, scrubbing the boots and the stand, but it was an experience that I relished. I enjoyed the freedom, responsibility and independence along with learning a trade and playing football every single day. I learned a lot over a short period.

It wasn't until I went there that it began to sink in that I was half-decent and had potential. It triggered something inside me to say 'look, it's time to take this more seriously'. I was training every day and it gave me a focus. My mindset was maturing, my self-belief growing.

We played Richmond in a pre-season friendly and the manager put me in, even though I was just 16 years old. I was way off the pace physically but I found I was able to drop into pockets of space, free from markers, and influenced the game that way.

▌THREE LIONS

Three months into my YTS I got asked to go for an England under-16 trial at Lilleshall with 50 others from around the country. I roomed with Paul Konchesky from Barking who was on the books at West Ham and Charlie MacDonald from Southwark who was with Charlton. They both oozed confidence, whereas I was from the smallest town on the planet and had never been to an Academy or a School of Excellence. I sat there, taken aback, listening and thinking 'what I am doing here?'

The first day we played against ourselves, teams against teams, 11 triallists versus 11 triallists. Despite my growing maturity at Darlington I reverted to my normal approach at trials of fading into the background. It was as though I didn't want to push myself in case I messed up or failed. I doubt the coaches noticed me; I must have been pretty anonymous. The ones who did well on the first day played academies the next day; the ones that were left over would play against themselves again. I was in the 'left-overs'.

I vividly remember the night before that 'left-overs' match. I'm not a religious person but, for some reason, I prayed that I would score a hat-trick the next day, partly because I thought that would be the only thing that would get me selected. Before then I had the self-belief that I could play but not enough confidence to come out of my shell, show others what I could do and stand out. However, the next day my prayers came true! I scored a hat-trick against Chris Kirkland and sparkled during the game. The coaches saw something in me and I got a letter through the post saying I'd been selected to play for England in Poland.

I'd never been close to playing for my country but I had a run of games, lining up and singing the National Anthem with the likes of Gareth Barry, Joe Cole, Leon

One of the most treasured possessions from my career. An England cap, signifying that I'd made it into an exclusive group.
© James Coppinger

Osman and Francis Jeffers, a lot of whom attended the Lilleshall School. We had an unbelievable team and, of course, they all went on to have unbelievable careers. What an experience, and, better still, it attracted attention from scouts that would turn my world upside down ...

THE NEXT BIG THING?

Although I'd only been at Darlington for seven or eight months my call-up for England under-16s placed me in the shop window. I heard some rumours that bigger clubs such as Newcastle United were showing interest but I never thought anything of them.

DEADLINE DAY

I went in for training as usual on transfer deadline day, and someone told me that the Darlington manager, David Hodgson, wanted to see me. You never went into the gaffer's office unless you had done something wrong and I just thought 'oh my God, what have I done? Have I not painted the dressing room right?!' I knocked on his door fearing the worst. Instead, he told me 'your dad is on his way down with your suit and you're to go to St James' Park to talk to Newcastle United. They want to sign you and Paul Robinson. So go up there, see what you can do, hopefully you can get something sorted.' I did a double-take. I just couldn't believe it. It was one of those moments that I never expected.

Mum and dad came to pick me up and we travelled the 37 miles to St James' Park. To get to the boardroom you go up in a big glass lift at the entrance which rises and reveals a panoramic view of Newcastle that takes the breath away. Well, at least it took our breath away. The two Darlington lads and our families, here to sign on the dotted line for Newcastle, could not have been more contrasting. I didn't know Paul Robinson but he was already a first-teamer at Darlington, born in Sunderland and the most confident, cocksure youngster you've ever met. Unlike me, he would have felt totally at ease if he had roomed with the likes of Konchesky and MacDonald at Lilleshall. His parents were also taking St James' Park in their stride. In contrast, there was James Coppinger and his mum and dad walking around with our mouths open like it was the first time we'd ever left Guisborough!

Russell Cushing was Newcastle's chief executive at the time and he put this eye-opening three-year contract in front of us. About £1,000 a week – compared to the YTS £42.50 a week I was on at Darlington – plus a £10,000 signing on fee. I thought 'oh my God this is unbelievable'. To get offered that sort of money felt ridiculous. I was blown away. I didn't have an agent at the time and my parents might have briefly considered pushing our luck and negotiating. But, in truth, Newcastle had us in the palm of their hands, and we didn't want to risk scuppering the deal. So we accepted the offer and I signed the contract whilst in a state of shock. The fee paid to Darlington, including add-ons, for Paul and myself was £1.8 million.

That night we went to my auntie's, who lived across the road in Guisborough, and had a party with

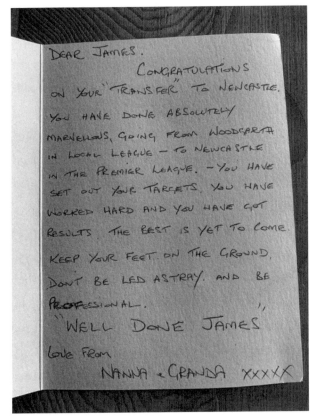

DEAR JAMES.
            CONGRATULATIONS
ON YOUR "TRANSFER" TO NEWCASTLE.
YOU HAVE DONE ABSOLUTELY
MARVELLOUS, GOING FROM WOODGARTH
IN LOCAL LEAGUE — TO NEWCASTLE
IN THE PREMIER LEAGUE. — YOU HAVE
SET OUT YOUR TARGETS. YOU HAVE
WORKED HARD AND YOU HAVE GOT
RESULTS THE BEST IS YET TO COME.
KEEP YOUR FEET ON THE GROUND,
DON'T BE LED ASTRAY. AND BE
PROFFESSIONAL.
"WELL DONE JAMES"
LOVE FROM
         NANNA & GRANDA xxxxx

Brilliant guidance that I'm not entirely sure I always followed.
© James Coppinger

family and friends. I remember opening all the cards congratulating me. It was surreal; a strange, strange feeling and although I was over the moon I already sensed that from now on I would be carrying a burden of expectations; to deliver on the pitch and live up to the Premier League lifestyle.

BIG TIME

The next day we went to the training ground at Chester-le-Street, met the manager, the legendary Scot, Kenny Dalglish, and trained with the first team. My mum, dad and sister came to watch.

Remember that it was less than a year since I had been playing Sunday League football with my mates and the day before I had been a YTS at Darlington. Now I was the 'next-big-thing'; a 17-year-old at a Premier League club that had just beaten the likes of Barcelona in the Champions League, in a city with an unbelievable appetite for football. The Geordies lived for Saturdays.

James Coppinger of Guisborough was now training with Alan Shearer, Gary Speed, Warren Barton, Robert Lee, John Barnes, Stuart Pearce and Ian Rush (plus Kenny Dalglish who joined in with the five-a-sides) – all players that I admired and looked up to. Pearce, who I'd watched play for England during that inspirational 1990 World Cup, was the first to come over. 'Psycho', as he was known, introduced himself, gripped me by the hand in his normal vice-like grip and wished me all the best for my career. My dad likes to tell the story that on that first day at Newcastle he gave me the advice that 'these blokes are professional footballers, don't try it on with them.' Then I nutmegged Psycho who nearly broke me in half the next time the ball came to me!

That first day was just a first-team taster. After that I normally trained with the under-17s in Durham, managed by John Carver. Whether I was training at Durham or Chester-le-Street or playing at St James' Park it felt like an honour to be there. The facilities were on a completely different level to what I'd known before. This was the big time.

When I started to train I saw that most weren't technically better than me, which was encouraging. Also, the fact that Newcastle had paid a fee for me helped me to feel like I justified being there. I didn't feel any pressure and just enjoyed it. Best of all, I bumped into Hoggy, the lad who had told me I'd never make it at the School of Excellence trial. I've always enjoyed proving people wrong and that felt good!

Off the pitch things happened quickly as I acquired some of the trappings of a professional footballer. As soon as I signed at Newcastle I got a nice sponsorship deal with Nike. I remember going to the factory with Grandad Herbert, who was 74 years old at the time. I can still see him, relishing every moment in his Nike tracksuit and cap! And agents started sniffing around. Sure enough, I signed up with one to handle my affairs.

But it didn't all go to my head. For a while I travelled to training from Guisborough to Durham by bus. I'd put my CD player on and relax. I had, though, purchased a brand new Citroen Saxo and after I passed my test it was ready for me, waiting on our drive, complete with its two years' free insurance! All the pros, even at youth level, were on good wages, and had decent cars. Yet I was still knocking about with my mates and living in Guisborough. I was at a Premier League club but, although everything was changing around me, I stayed the same.

RUUD GULLIT AND ALAN IRVINE

At the end of the 1997/98 season, Newcastle finished 13th in the Premier League and lost in the FA Cup Final to Arsenal. At the start of the next, after a poor start, Sir Kenny Dalglish was sacked and replaced by Dutchman Ruud Gullit.

Meanwhile, back in the youth set-up, my development went through the roof that season. I was now mainly working with Alan Irvine, who managed the under-19s, and he helped me get better and better. I was still in that honeymoon period of having signed for a Premier League club, loving my football, loving going to train, loving wearing all the Nike gear. There weren't any negatives.

Irvine was a driving force and imposed incredibly professional standards. You had to be on it. Every day. There was nowhere to hide. You couldn't get away with anything. We had structure and I always reacted well to structure. In the Youth Cup we beat Chelsea at Stamford Bridge in extra time, beat Nottingham Forest at the City Ground and then beat Middlesbrough at the Riverside. Our winning run only came to an end in the semi-finals where we lost against Coventry over two legs. Irvine was tactically astute and he employed a diamond formation with me in a kind of number-ten role which suited me perfectly.

I loved it; trying to find spaces and get into holes where I was difficult to mark. Before the ball came to me I had a picture in my mind of who was around me and thoughts on what I was going to do. It was like I was constantly solving puzzles, playing things out in my brain before the ball arrived, so I could receive it on the half-turn and play people through on goal.

That's a characteristic that's quite rare and difficult to coach and I got satisfaction out of being admired and appreciated as a smart, clever footballer who could read the game.

Alan Irvine – stopwatch in hand, meticulous as ever.
© Newcastle United Football Club

I sometimes got called up to join the reserves, and when the first team got to the FA Cup Final against

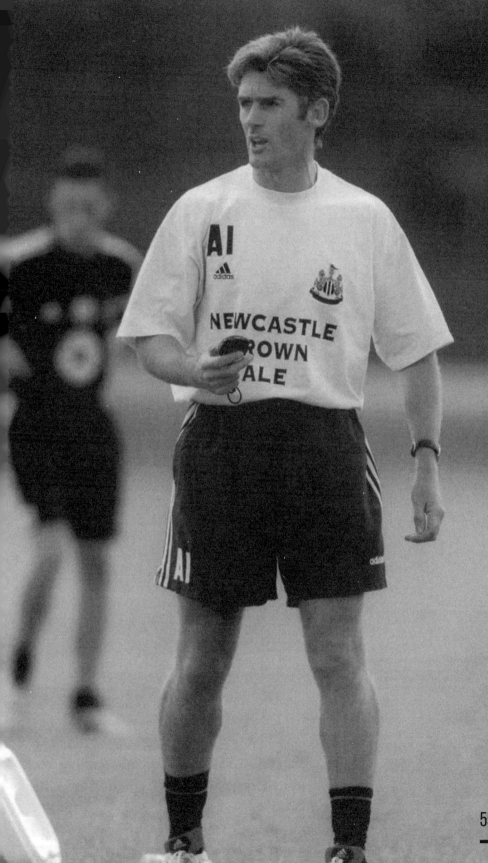

In action for Newcastle's youth team.

© Newcastle United Football Club

Manchester United, I thought I had a sniff of getting into the squad. Instead, I watched at Wembley as the team were runners-up for a consecutive season. Gullit's first season precisely matched Dalglish's last, with the team also finishing 13th in the Premier League again.

SIR BOBBY, HARTLEPOOL AND A PREMIER LEAGUE DEBUT

To my surprise, Ruud included me in the senior squad that went to Holland, Scotland and Germany to play pre-season friendlies. I partnered Alan Shearer up front in some of the games, and, in one, when Shearer had come off, I took the penalty. All very promising, but it became clear that physically I was way off it. Even in pre-season I just ran out of steam and energy. I specifically remember being in Scotland and realising that my body was nowhere near conditioned to play senior football. At 18 years old, with a youth's physique, it was just too early for me.

Ruud Gullit had an uncompromising style and locked horns with some of the senior players. Rob Lee, who had been club captain, and Stuart Pearce were ostracised from the senior squad and not even allocated a squad number at the start of the 1999/2000 season. In contrast, I was given 26 and retained that shirt number throughout my career.

Four games into the season the conflict came to a head when Gullit took the controversial decision to put both Alan Shearer (widely seen as the 'main man' at the club) and Duncan Ferguson on the bench for a crucial Tyne-Wear derby against Sunderland at St James' Park. Instead, Paul Robinson, who had transferred with me from Darlington, started as the striker in a 2-1 defeat.

That defeat against the local rivals proved to be the end for Ruud. Having fallen out with fans' favourites it was never going to end well for him unless he won every game, and after the Sunderland defeat he was replaced by Sir Bobby Robson.

Of course, Sir Bobby had been the England manager during the 1990 World Cup that I found so inspirational. Now some nine years later he was managing my club! However, any initial warmth that I felt was quickly replaced by shock as one of his first acts was to put the whole reserve team squad, myself included, on the transfer list! It was an absolute bolt out of the blue. I spoke to my dad on the phone, got upset and cried. It was the first time since I had been at the club that I had experienced anything of this sort, and I remember thinking 'oh my God what am I going to do?' I'd never thought about leaving Newcastle and was worried.

■ MAN ON A MISSION

What was Sir Bobby up to? I talked to Alan Irvine and John Carver to try to get a better understanding. Their view was that it was a scare tactic to liven the older players who had got too comfortable and complacent in the reserves. They didn't think I was specifically targeted; however, they advised me to 'go on loan, have a good spell and see if the gaffer likes you'. So, a few months later, I used it as a springboard to go out and get my first taste of first-team pro football at Hartlepool. I went there on a mission, thinking 'I'm gonna have to go out and prove myself here.'

Newcastle United squad photo. I'm second row, far right of the players, alongside some Premier League legends. Did I ever really believe I belonged?

© Newcastle United Football Club

It was a good decision. Coincidentally, Mark Robinson, who I grew up with, was there, pushing to get into the first team, and I knew a few of the others, such as Graeme Lee. I scored on my professional debut against Barnet and relished turning up on a Saturday and winning a football match. Experiencing that addictive feeling was an eye-opener. I saw how much it meant to the players and supporters and enjoyed the atmosphere in the dressing room with a really good set of players that wanted to do well. I loved it and wanted more. In total I played in ten games, scoring three goals, and we sneaked into the play-offs on the final day of the season at Exeter. Unfortunately, we missed out in the semi-final against Darlington but I returned to Newcastle having grown up a bit, become a better player and with a real desire to push on in the next season.

▍BURPEES WITH BOBBY

There's a photo of Newcastle United's first-team squad before the start of the 2000/01 season, and alongside

Sir Bobby Robson, there are legends such as Alan Shearer, Gary Speed, Rob Lee, Kieron Dyer, Duncan Ferguson and Shay Given. And, tucked into the far-right corner of the second row, there I am. I was back at Newcastle, itching to prove that I was ready and good enough.

Funnily enough, I partnered Sir Bobby in some of the pre-season conditioning sessions, doing sit-ups, burpees and press-ups. He was 67 years of age by then and wanted to keep in shape so would be doing them as well. I'd be counting, and everyone would be watching and laughing while I tried to keep a straight face. Sir Bobby was quite a character. In the team meetings he would forget everybody's name and have people in stitches, but we were all laughing with him rather than at him. That said, it would have been unwise to underestimate him or take advantage. He was no one's fool. He could be ruthless and stern, as I would find out.

You could see why Alan Shearer and the senior pros warmed to him. He had this ability to get the best out of them. He was so authentic and real, with an aura and personality that everyone immediately warmed to. He was great to be around. Everybody bought into what he did.

By this time he had been a successful manager of England and also achieved a lot at clubs such as Ipswich Town and Barcelona. He had nothing left to prove – yet he had lost none of his energy and enthusiasm for the game. He was obsessed. 100 per cent committed. Living each day at 100 miles an hour (he used to get his haircut in the changing room to save time). Every single day he would give everything and you believed everything he said because of that passion. A football man through and through to his core. Sadly, it wasn't long after he moved into retirement that his health deteriorated. He needed football as much as it needed him.

STARS

It wasn't only the manager at Newcastle who was a star. Many of the players were also household names and I was still a little awestruck in their company.

The much-missed Gary Speed was an inspiration for me. I watched him every day, the way he went about his business, how happy and jovial he was. The standards he set for himself and everyone else were impressive.

As an aside, nearly ten years later I played against Gary in an FA Cup tie when I was at Doncaster Rovers and he was at Bolton Wanderers. After the game he took the time and trouble to sit down and have a chat in the players' lounge. He didn't know me that well and I was flattered. A classy act that I tried to emulate.

The inspirational and much-missed, Gary Speed. A class act.
© Newcastle United Football Club

I loved the big Scot Duncan Ferguson and got on well with him. He was an £8 million signing from Everton and a star but great with the youngsters. I remember in pre-season we were all putting in the hard yards on the running track and he warned us that 'if anybody goes past me I'm gonna give him a clip!' So six of us queued up behind him, too scared to overtake. That story is misleading though. People looked at this 6ft 4in, fearless, powerhouse of a centre-forward – but that wasn't the whole story because off the pitch he was one of the nicest men you've come across. He loved a game of pool, and I was disappointed when he returned to Everton at the start of that season.

Alan Shearer was another fantastic guy who led by example; and what a striker; the most clinical one I ever played with. His goalscoring record speaks for itself.

I cleaned John Barnes's boots and he was also absolutely class with me.

What resonated with me was that they were all human beings! I'd seen them on the telly and thought of them almost as aliens, from another planet. Whereas when I got to meet them, became part of their circle and trained with them I realised they were made from normal flesh and blood.

▌PREMIER LEAGUE DEBUT

Soon I wasn't just sharing a training pitch with those stars but the hallowed turf of St James' Park. I impressed Bobby Robson in pre-season to such a degree that I was included in the match-day squad and made my

Daniel Cordone off, James Coppinger on. My one and only experience in the Premier League.
© Newcastle United Football Club

Newcastle United and Premier League debut as a 79th-minute substitute against Tottenham Hotspur.

Funnily enough, the image from that day that remains clearest in my mind is when I went to press Stephen Carr, who played right-back for Tottenham, down in the corner near his goal-line. I had two options: let him clear it down the line, potentially to one of our players, or close him down, block the clearance and allow them to get a throw in. For whatever reason, I decided to let him clear it down the line. He found a Tottenham shirt and they ended up 'getting out' and moving up the pitch. Sir Bobby went mad at me on the touchline.

I'm not saying that it would have changed my career if I'd have made a different choice with Stephen Carr and impressed Sir Bobby, but sometimes football (and life) is all about small margins and 'sliding door' moments that change everything. If I had made a better impression in those 15 minutes I genuinely feel like things could have turned out differently.

For instance, a couple of weeks later another young player, Shola Ameobi, made his debut against Chelsea and ended up having a fracas with Chelsea's fiery Dennis Wise where he stood his ground and got praise from everyone. A couple of games later he scored and, building on that excellent start, went on to play more than 300 games for Newcastle. Small margins.

Not that I felt downhearted after the Tottenham game. Far from it. Alan Shearer spoke to my dad afterwards and said, 'He's got a chance, he's gonna have a fantastic career if he keeps going and keeps doing what he's doing.' And not long after my initial three-year contract was extended by another three years. All was good. This felt like just the beginning. It felt like I'd made it. How little I knew.

PREMIER LEAGUE PLAYER, UNIVERSITY STUDENT LIFESTYLE

That taster against Tottenham was a memorable day and a fantastic achievement for a 19-year-old. Breaking into the first team match-day squad and getting minutes on the pitch could have been a stepping stone in my career. Unfortunately, I just wasn't mature enough and mentally ready to push on.

After the likes of Gary Caldwell, Steve Caldwell and Shola Ameobi made their first-team debut they became more focused and driven. Not me. I doubt it was Shearer's kind words but after the game I thought I'd cracked it and became complacent. I stopped doing the things that got me to that point. I'd always been opinionated and stubborn but now I took that up a notch. I thought I had the right to question everything and to blame everybody else if things went wrong. I got a bit 'big time' and too big for my boots, which was a massive error.

▌'WHO DO YOU THINK YOU ARE?'

Sir Bobby soon picked up on that. He collared me and made an example of me. After my debut, I went out and bought a brand new BMW Z3. I think the security guards at the Chester-le-Street training ground thought I was one of the regular first-team players, so one morning they told me to park next to Sir Bobby's car. We'd gone out to warm up around the

Sir Bobby – a legend of the game. An inspirational and charming man but strict as well, as I found to my cost.

© Newcastle United Football Club

track, right next to where the cars were parked, and he asked, 'Whose car is that?' I put my hand up and he grilled me: 'Who do you think you are? My son works in a factory, nine 'til five, every single day. You've made one appearance and you think you've made it?'

I was so embarrassed and felt belittled in front of the first team. I thought it was a little bit harsh at the time but I look back now and he was spot on. It was like he was issuing a warning: 'Don't get ahead of yourself. Don't get flash. Stay grounded and work hard.' I soon sold the car. Every time I got in it after that I didn't feel like I deserved it.

That was typical of Sir Bobby. Yes, he had his quirks and foibles that made people laugh but he could be strict. I think it was the way he was conditioned and brought up in football. When he played he was probably treated harshly, because the majority of the managers back then were disciplinarians. There was no point in answering back; you had to just accept it and get on with it.

In truth, I think he rated me. He once described me to the media as having the potential to become the new Zola (Gianfranco Zola the brilliant Italian who mainly played for Chelsea and became one of the Premier League's finest-ever players) and two or three years later when I was at Doncaster a mutual friend told me that he always asked about me.

Despite the putdown, I retained total respect for him. The next day he had moved on and treated me no differently because he never held a grudge, not least because when he issued the dressing down it was because he thought it would be for my long-term benefit.

Yet despite Robson's guidance I lost my way. People were in my ear, telling me that I was this and that, and I ended up believing the hype, which was very sad, not least because my new-found sense of self-importance affected some relationships at the club.

I fell out with Sir Bobby's assistant manager Mick Wadsworth and didn't feature during the season after that. I never got on with Mick. He was old-school and hard with the younger players. If you couldn't cope with it – which I couldn't a lot of the time – then that was a problem because Mick wasn't changing. I struggled to play and train in his company because as soon as I made any sort of mistake he'd be down on me like a tonne of bricks.

Nobody else made me feel like that. Although Alan Irvine and John Carver were also both strict they had more warmth. Looking back I don't think Mick was authentic or real in his approach. I think like he felt he had to act that way, rather than really wanting to.

It didn't help that I was a very poor communicator, with slouched and negative body language, little eye contact, but plenty of opinions which I was keen to share. I always thought I was right. No wonder I came across as arrogant (though that was just a front that camouflaged my fears and anxieties), no wonder I struggled to build relationships with coaches and managers. I'm not sure if word of my moaning got back to Mick or whether he overheard anything, but, if so, it wouldn't have helped.

Since those days I've learned so much about the importance of posture, facial expressions, listening and how to speak to people – and have been able to build really strong relationships with many different coaches and managers at Doncaster. Now, armed with that knowledge, I can confidently state the 19-year-old me was a shocking communicator!

At that stage of my career I always felt, for whatever reason, that people in authority, such as managers and coaches, disliked me and I got into the bad habit of criticising and blaming others. I recently read an article that was written when I first joined Doncaster, and in it I blamed Sir Bobby Robson, blamed the coaches, blamed all the bad luck I'd had for why my career had gone off-track. I came across as a victim. The only person I didn't blame was me! I had no accountability and a bad attitude.

BAD HABITS, LOW STANDARDS

For the 2000/01 season I trained and played with the reserves who were managed by Tommy Craig. In the reserves there is often a mix: some players have had a taste of first-team football but have dropped down and don't want to be there, then there are ambitious 18- and 19-year-olds who are coming through the ranks from youth teams where they've been used to playing competitive games.

In between the first-team and the youth set-up, the reserves can be a bit of nothingness. We had a core of eight or nine of us and the culture was a bit too relaxed and comfortable. In training we very rarely had two goalkeepers so we did a lot of small-sided keep-ball games involving a lot of tippy-tappy football. The intensity wasn't there. We never really had a purpose because the games were sporadic and didn't mean much, a bit like under-23 games in modern-day football. When there was a game we tended to overplay, with too many touches on the ball, and our tempo was poor.

Generally, standards weren't high, which was no kind of preparation for the Premier League and it created a lot of bad habits; on and off the pitch, mentally, physically and technically. Under Tommy's laid-back approach I didn't develop, didn't get the best out of myself – and I started to do things differently off the pitch as well.

CHOCOLATE AND BINGE-DRINKING

Twenty years ago the whole concept of professionalism within football was very different. For instance, at Newcastle we had bowls of chocolate bars available to us whenever we wanted them. That wasn't good for me because it's always been my guilty food pleasure and something I crave. As a kid I started my love affair with Terry's Chocolate Orange, the one with the segments. They never lasted long. And at Newcastle chocolate was always there if you wanted it, potentially washed down with cans of coke. That's just how it was then. Even away from the club I wasn't eating the right foods, partly because I had no understanding of what the right foods were.

Attitudes towards drinking were also very different

in English football 20 years ago. There was a drinking culture at many clubs, including Newcastle, and my socialising habits became harmful. It probably didn't help that I bought a flat on the quayside in Newcastle and shared my time between there and Guisborough. Newcastle had a buzzing nightlife and I was always out with friends and teammates. I almost lived a university student lifestyle and didn't take the responsibilities of my job seriously.

On Saturday nights you could guarantee that the players would meet up and go out around the town – and it wasn't just for a few drinks. We'd be binge drinking until three/four o'clock in the morning. Maybe we'd be out on Sundays as well, and there would be 'team-bonding' sessions on a Tuesday night. The majority of the squad would be there, albeit some drinking more than others, some knowing when to stop.

There were a few who could cope with this punishing schedule of socialising and drinking and were pretty unaffected. They could still perform in training and games, but it eventually caught up with most and performances dropped as they weren't getting the rest they needed, weren't hydrating correctly and weren't maintaining peak fitness.

I sort of convinced myself that it would be all right and I could do it but, in truth, it affected me physically and mentally. Alcohol has never suited me. It's a depressant and it affected me badly. I enjoyed going out and wanted to be part of the in-crowd, but it undoubtedly had a detrimental effect on my football and my mental health.

▍HEART-BREAK

I'm not making excuses for my lifestyle choices at that time, but, looking back, some personal circumstances didn't help. Professional footballers are also human beings and just as affected by events in their personal lives as the rest of society.

Around this time I had to deal with a lot off the pitch. To start, my parents were going through a divorce. We were a really happy family and then, one day, my mum left and my dad found it tough. It was really difficult for me to understand. They separated just as I signed at St James' Park, so I no longer had the stable family home that I loved so much to go back to. It never felt the same after that, and perhaps that induced me to move out earlier than I would have done and relocate to Newcastle.

I also had bereavement and grief to deal with. If my mum or dad was working Grandad Herbert would step in and take me to games. I went to a few trials with him and people would say 'Is that your dad?' and that would make him feel good. He had an infectious enthusiasm for football and life and was always so proud of my football achievements. He inspired me and was arguably the biggest, or one of the biggest, driving forces in me being successful and maintaining belief in myself. I was so close to him and he told me that I was 'the apple of his eye' – so it was heart-breaking to watch this super-fit 74-year-old be diagnosed with cancer (he was unable to come to my Premier League debut because he wasn't well enough), deteriorate for nine months and then to be at his bedside in his room as he passed away.

I literally watched him die in front of me and I struggled to believe it, understand it or process it for several years.

I had lost one of my biggest inspirations, my hero, at an age when I was already feeling overwhelmed by all that was going on. He left a massive gap and though it's difficult to measure I suspect the grief affected my confidence and my well-being. I didn't know what to do and I'm sure some of my excessive socialising was a way of masking the sorrow.

■ 'YOU'LL GROW'

The 2000/01 season had started so promisingly with that debut against Tottenham. Yet, instead of establishing myself in the first team, I went out of favour and spent it with the reserves where I lost my edge and got bored.

I still had more than a year on my contract but by now it was clear to me that I wasn't motivated to play for Newcastle just for the prestige. I never wanted the tag of 'professional footballer' or to be able to say 'I play for Newcastle United' if it meant going through the motions in the reserves. No, I wanted to try to carve out a long-term career in pro football somewhere where I could get game time, play in the first team every Saturday, make a difference and win things.

I booked an appointment through Sir Bobby Robson's secretary to discuss my future. Typically, because he was always operating at 100 miles an hour and doing more than one thing at a time, he spoke to me as he was getting changed, washing his face in the sink.

He asked me, 'How old are you son?' I said 'I'm 20 Gaffer,' and he said, 'You'll grow.' He was always telling me that. He said he didn't want me to go on loan and preferred to keep me at the club; that I was only young, this, that and the other, but it washed over me because I couldn't see myself at Newcastle anymore. I wanted to play first-team football and make a difference and so I almost forced myself out.

HARTLEPOOL, AGAIN

In 2001/02 I went back to Hartlepool on loan again. Again it was successful. I scored on my debut against Rushden and Diamonds in a 5-1 win and made 14 appearances, scoring two goals and helping them to the play-offs. I liked the responsibility of being a Premier League player operating in Division Three and knew I was good enough to stand out at that level.

With the contract at Newcastle beginning to come to an end, I hoped to be offered something by Hartlepool. I had a meeting with Chris Turner, the manager, who said, 'If we get through the play-offs and get promoted we'll sign you, but if we don't, we won't because we feel like you're better than this level and we don't feel like your style of play suits Division Three.' I didn't know where to go with that, to be honest.

Unfortunately, they lost in the play-offs and in the wake of ITV Digital's collapse they were unable to offer me a contract. I would need to look elsewhere to kick start my stalling career …

EYEWITNESS

ALAN IRVINE

From now on in the book we will occasionally pause to get a different perspective – independently gathered – on my story and the importance of mindset from someone who has been involved in my career.

Who better to start with than Alan Irvine, a proper football man. He played as a winger for Queen's Park, Everton, Crystal Palace, Dundee United and Blackburn Rovers before becoming a coach. He worked at Blackburn Rovers and Preston North End before our paths crossed at Newcastle United where he was a manager with the youth team.

I found him to be strict, straightforward and fair, demanding high standards every day. I learned a lot and loved playing for him.

Since then he has coached and managed at Everton, Preston, Sheffield Wednesday, West Bromwich Albion, Blackburn, Norwich City and West Ham United, where he is employed at the time of writing.

ASSETS AND ATTITUDE – 'When he came to Newcastle from Darlington James was signed as a young player with a lot of potential. I always felt that his biggest assets were his positional intelligence and understanding of the role. He was technically very gifted.

'It's no surprise to me that, all these years on, he's doing a book with a different slant rather than the normal "let's tell a few stories". What you don't know is what the boys are doing away from the club – which is most of their time – but I would certainly never have questioned James's attitude. I had absolutely no feeling that he was unprofessional. Sometimes you will hear and suspect things, but I didn't with James.'

ADJUSTING TO A PREMIER LEAGUE CLUB – 'I've seen players who have a problem adapting to their surroundings. It doesn't surprise me to learn that James never felt that he deserved to be at Newcastle because Darlington to Newcastle is a big, big step up.

'I know because I did it myself. I went from Queens Park in the Scottish Second Division to Everton. My last game for Queens Park was against Cowdenbeath; my first for Everton was against Inter Milan. I was older than James when I moved and I'm not sure I could have coped with it at a younger age. I was 21 and I always felt I was only visiting, thinking "I won't be here for very long. I'll do three years and then I'll go back to being an insurance broker."

'We didn't look at him at the time and think he wasn't ready to meet this step. We felt he had the qualities; he was a gifted footballer and was able to cope from a football point of view.'

TRYING TO BECOME ESTABLISHED AT NEWCASTLE – 'I always felt it was going to be difficult for James to make it right at the very top level, but always believed that he was strong enough to have a successful career and I don't think anybody would dispute that he's achieved that.

'Bear in mind that the team James was trying to get into at Newcastle had top, top internationals. He was competing with an incredibly high standard, some of the best strikers that have been around. Duncan Ferguson: 6ft 4in, fantastic technically and could run. Alan Shearer: one of the best strikers there has ever been. Pace and power, particularly as a younger player before he had injuries and had to adapt his game. A world-class striker, extremely strong, great finisher. James was competing against that level of striker so he would have needed to be exceptional to break through.'

PACE AND POWER – 'I could look at every young player that I've ever worked with in youth set-ups and pinpoint their strengths – the reason they got to that level – and the things that might stop them from making the next step.

'You can hide some weaknesses if they are strong in other areas. Jamie Vardy can hide weaknesses in his game because of that fantastic pace that he's got. Michail Antonio doesn't have James's technical ability, doesn't have James's positional understanding but he's extremely effective because he's an absolute powerhouse.

'James lacked the physicality that was probably going to be needed to be a striker in the Premier League. He wasn't big and strong and he wasn't rapid. It doesn't mean everyone has to be exceptionally strong or quick but if you're not then you have to be exceptionally gifted. David Silva, for example, played at the highest level because he was truly exceptional at the other parts of his game. Or a Bernardo Silva or Phil Foden. You look at Raheem Sterling who would be James's size – I wouldn't say he has better awareness but he's much stronger and quicker.

'However, James still played at a very good level because he's been able to use his brains, his technical ability and his awareness.'

RESERVE-TEAM FOOTBALL – 'A lot of young boys do well as youth players, make progress and play the right level of football to continue to stretch and challenge them, without overdoing it and eroding their confidence.

'The problem comes if they don't get into the first team and become too old for the youth teams set up. Then they fall between teams and their development reaches a plateau and actually tails off because they're not being getting stretched in the way that they need to be stretched. They've had proper squad-based training and now suddenly the coaches have got a real challenge to keep developing them, without enough players to work with. There might only be a group of three, four or five.

'Lads are extremely well looked after at Academy level, up until they're under-18s. Everything is done for them and there are education and welfare officers and all that kind of stuff. At first-team level they are pampered. Everything is done for them as well. But that group in the middle can be forgotten.'

MINDSET – 'Professional footballers are challenged week in, week out. They have to cope with setbacks, rise above them and move on to the next game, or even move on within that particular game. One of the things I've always said is that Premier League players are almost all bomb-proof. They make a mistake that you think is absolutely obvious to everybody and a lot of them just shrug their shoulders and get on with it. Mental toughness is huge and the whole mental side of the game is enormous. I'm not just talking about resilience but professionalism, game understanding and intelligence.

'James has had a lot of highs and lows during his career. He's had promotions and relegations and needed to be able to bounce back. And he had to get to the stage where he recognised that "I'm actually good enough to play at a very good level".'

IF I KNEW THEN ...

In the previous few chapters I've gone into detail on my time at Newcastle because I think it's an interesting case study that many young footballers will be able to relate to. They may face similar challenges and feel similar emotions.

Now, more than 20 years after my departure from Newcastle, it's worth pausing to reflect on what went right and what went wrong, not least because the challenges and obstacles I faced in trying to establish myself have been and will be repeated many, many times.

When these kinds of opportunities arise, I want others to be better equipped to cope with it than I was.

OPPORTUNITY OF A LIFETIME

What's clear is that I had an opportunity that doesn't come around very often. If I could have become a first-team regular at Newcastle there would've been the potential to test myself with and against the best of the best, in one of the big five, top-tier football leagues in Europe, along with Germany, Spain, Italy and France.

I'd have played each week in front of massive crowds and global television audiences, and I would have earned life-changing amounts of money. The average salary for a Premier League player at the time of my debut was around £450,000 a year and over the next ten years that increased to £1.1 million.

To perform in the Premier League for years like Gareth Barry (a record 653 Premier League appearances), Ryan Giggs and James Milner requires an all-consuming obsession that I'm not entirely sure I could have matched. Yet many people have told me that I should have played at a higher level for longer, and they may be right. If only I'd been in the right headspace and had the right guidance and support.

Upon reflection, I think that for much of my time at Newcastle my career was on track and in line with the path that the club intended for me. In the first few months I settled in the under-17s. During the 1998/99 season I starred for the under-19s in the Youth Cup and improved under Alan Irvine. In 1999/00, when Sir Bobby Robson took over at the club, I went on loan to Hartlepool and benefitted from my first taste of professional football. And I returned in 2000/01, as a 19-year-old who had done enough to be selected in a match-day squad in the Premier League. Not many 19-year-olds reach that level so quickly, so whilst I had much to learn and many areas where I could develop, up until that point my future at St James' looked bright.

But it was my technical and tactical skills that had got me that far. My physique and, particularly, my mindset were not Premier League standard. I've learned not to have regrets but if I'd had known then what I know now – or to be more precise, to think the way I now think – then it might have been a different story.

Perhaps the height of my Newcastle career was the moment before I allowed Tottenham's Stephen Carr to clear that ball down the line. After that my reputation within the club gradually began to fall and the opportunity to become established in the first team slipped through my fingers. My potential wasn't fulfilled.

■ 'WHY AM I HERE?'

So what were the issues and obstacles that got in the way?

Without a doubt I took my small town, Sunday League mentality to the club. I felt lucky to be there and overawed by my surroundings, the ambitions and the expectancy of the club.

I'd like to say it was a dream come true but it wasn't something that I ever really dreamt about. I didn't have any awareness or understanding of the behaviour expected of a pro footballer. I was described as one on my contract but that never really sunk in. It never felt like a proper job and I still knocked about with my mates.

This was reflected in my lack of confidence. Even though I made progress through the under-17s and 19s, and despite my strong-willed outward demeanour, I questioned whether I was good enough.

- Why did Kenny Dalglish sign me?
- Why am I here?
- Why have they chosen me to play for Newcastle when there are so many good players in the youth team?
- Why did Bobby Robson give me my debut?

I was always fighting these sort of doubts and criticism from managers and coaches (and some comments from other players) reinforced them.

A big part of the barrier that I put up was due to my physicality. I suffered self-doubt after I got rejected from trials because I was judged to be too small. The average height of players at professional football clubs was around 5ft 11in. I was four inches shorter. Add in that fact that most were heavier and more muscular led to a lingering feeling – that I never really lost – that I was always at a physical disadvantage. Certainly, I was conscious that to play in the Premier League you need to be either small and incredibly pacey or tall and strong. I was neither; and although I managed my game to get the best out of my attributes, the thought was always nagging away at the back of my mind.

It's been interesting to read Alan Irvine's words in the eyewitness chapter supporting this view – and with such strong competition for places at Newcastle it was always likely to be an uphill struggle to establish myself in the Premier League. Perhaps that's why I felt like a bit of an imposter.

Looking back, though, I think I was a bit hard on myself. Firstly, most young players would have questioned whether they belonged at a club of Newcastle's stature and whether they deserved to play football in the company of the likes of Shearer and Speed, Lee and Dyer. It was perfectly normal to feel a bit overwhelmed and overawed and, besides, in some ways I was right: I wasn't anywhere near their standard. But I realise now that I wasn't supposed to be. I was work in progress and had time on my side. I'm not sure that I fully understood that at 19 years old I didn't have to be the finished article.

FOLLOWING THE FLOCK

Another obstacle was that I wasn't strong enough to take accountability and make my own decisions. I was a sheep; too happy to follow the flock, too easily influenced by others. I allowed my standards to drop when I was in the reserves, I allowed myself to get drawn into the drinking culture when I knew it was bad for me, I allowed criticism and insults to affect my confidence. I was scared about what people would say, so I chose not to do extra, chose not to be in the gym, and chose not to work harder. Simply, because it wasn't seen as cool.

Instead, I always gravitated to the ones who weren't putting the work in. I just trained, got in my car, drove home and then went out with my teammates or friends and socialised. I was living a normal life whilst being contracted to a Premier League football club. I wasn't preparing properly for training or matches, or recovering properly afterwards. I wasn't eating or hydrating properly. I wasn't doing enough off the pitch. All of this because I wasn't strong enough mentally to have the guts and self-discipline to act more professionally, even though, deep down, I wanted to.

That was the teenage me in a nutshell. I was always so worried about what people thought of me that I effectively let other people make decisions that affected my life. In short, I prioritised being popular with the in-crowd in the Newcastle dressing room above my performance on the pitch. These were all unwise choices even if they weren't consciously made. It wasn't that I deliberately chose to follow a certain path, I just didn't think about it.

■ MINDSET

Ultimately, it was my mindset that let me down. I was young and lacked confidence, and maturity. I didn't see football as a job, didn't apply myself as well as I should have done, didn't seize the moment and grasp the opportunity.

I was unconsciously influencing my thinking with who I was hanging around with, and at the time I didn't know how to control that. A lot of people were clinging on to me because they thought I was 'the next big thing'. I wasn't. I had made one fleeting appearance but people perceived me that way. In short, I wasn't mentally prepared and can't believe I got to where I got to, thinking the way I was.

For balance, I should say that I was always a team-player who always put in the effort at training and on a match-day. However, I had zero self-awareness and understanding that I had the potential to improve my thinking patterns. If I had thought about it all – which I didn't – I would have said that mindset was something you were born with, not something you could change. I was oblivious to the fact that the way I thought – my 'mind-map' – was affecting everything I was doing. If I had known at the age of 19 the kind of mental skills that I later developed, then I would have coped better and given myself a much better chance of playing the bulk of my pro career in the Premier League. I now know that you have to take ownership of everything if you want to be successful. You have to understand what it takes.

At the time of writing I have been mentoring someone who was released by a Premier League club and he was blaming other people and said that he hadn't stood a chance. Nothing was his fault, but then in the same breath he admitted he could have done more. That's exactly where I was myself when I wasn't self-aware and wasn't thinking in helpful ways.

■ 'WHAT DO WE DO NOW?'

In truth, I desperately needed help at Newcastle to show me the way forward, because I didn't know what I was doing or where I was going. This was new territory for me and, at times, I felt disorientated and out of my depth.

Because I didn't take the initiative myself I would've benefitted from having a mentor or role model who could have guided me and put me back on track. An expert who had been there, done it and got the T-shirt would have been priceless. Sadly, that wasn't the case.

Just to be clear I'm not blaming anybody and, in particular, I don't want to do my parents a disservice. They didn't know any different. They had been conditioned by their parents who were normal people, working nine to five, living for the weekend. So when their son started playing for Newcastle they were like 'what do we do now?'

It didn't help that Mum and Dad were in the process of divorce. My mum didn't want to give me any bad advice because she'd just left – and my dad had his own troubles to deal with. He wasn't sure what was best for me. To be fair he used to say to me all the time, 'Do you realise where you are and what you're doing?' and I just used to think 'what is he talking about?' and laugh it off.

Also, I no longer had Grandad Herbert's positive influence. He used to tell me to avoid girlfriends, drinking and partying but, sadly, that guidance and support could no longer be heard.

ROLE MODELS

That said, with the benefit of hindsight I realise that if I had been on the lookout there were mentors and role models all around me who could have helped me if I had asked. Alan Irvine was the epitome of a professional coach, and there was the example of Gary Speed and Alan Shearer, to name but two, in the senior squad. I would've just needed to watch and copy them.

Within my age group I had always played with the likes of Gary and Stevie Caldwell and Aaron Hughes. That was the group I needed to join, the example I needed to follow. They weren't technically outstanding but worked incredibly hard at their game. They were ultra-professional and level headed. They put in extra hours on the training pitch, ate and drank the right things, listened to the coaches, and always strove to get better.

Aaron Hughes – 112 international and 455 Premier League appearances. He was a potential role model for me if I had been aware of the opportunity.
© Newcastle United Football Club

However, I became part of a circle that would hammer them, criticise them and laugh and joke at their expense. We'd say, 'They're busy' (uncool and trying too hard). I used to think 'I don't want to work harder because people will hammer me.' I worked fairly hard in training but I could have done more.

The Caldwell's parents were a driving force; supportive, giving them clear direction and focus. They had it all planned out for them, always thinking ahead, making sure they were on track, giving them the best possible chance of success. All the family in harmony with a common goal to make the best of their career.

Subsequently, Aaron Hughes played 455 Premier League games and 112 caps for Northern Ireland. Gary Caldwell played 356 games (mainly for Hibernian, Celtic and Wigan) as well as 55 times for Scotland, and Steven played 369 games, with 12 appearances for Scotland. What unbelievable careers! They have my full respect and admiration. So, I wish I'd have followed their path sooner. Essentially, in their teenage years they already had the professional mindset that I'd later acquire. Like me, they had a fantastic opportunity at Newcastle – and they made the most of it.

⌈ANALYSIS⌋

SELF-BELIEF AND CONFIDENCE

Along with a love for the game, I would say that self-belief and confidence ('having a positive view of yourself and what you can do') is the most important quality that a footballer can have – and the story of my time at Newcastle underlines that point.

Like me, most young (and not so young) footballers' confidence goes up when they play well and receive praise, and drops when they play badly and get criticised. The same is also true of teams. When they win self-belief grows, but when they are on a losing run it falls away.

It doesn't have to be like this. Confidence isn't something that has to go up and down depending on results and other people's opinions. If I hear that a player is 'just lacking confidence' I think

> 'Belief is the most important thing in football. Not quality, running or being strong but belief, faith and fight'
>
> **Mauricio Pochettino**

that's an excuse. With practice and a strong mentality, it's possible to build confidence that is pretty high all the time and doesn't go up and down so wildly in line with events.

The most mentally strong players don't lose confidence when things go wrong. They know that everyone makes mistakes and that they are a great way to learn. They know that as a professional footballer they will come under scrutiny from managers, coaches, supporters and the media, and are an easy target for criticism and moaning. They know it's impossible to please everyone and be universally popular. So they keep trying to improve, maintain the highest standards and keep the faith.

I tell all the kids that I coach now that you should believe that you're the best player in the team. I always thought like that. That doesn't mean getting in other people's faces, being boastful and telling them 'I'm better than you'. It's just about believing in yourself and that you can achieve anything that you want to achieve.

Confidence and belief are massive.

▊FORM

The whole concept of being in or out of form is an interesting one. It's a commonly used phrase in sport and suggests someone or a team is on a good or bad run. The problem with form is that when there has been a series of poor performances or defeats then we can create a concept in our mind of being in a slump and our confidence and self-belief can dip. The more importance we apply to this 'slump' then the more difficult it is to get out of it.

'You have to have faith in your own qualities; that is part of being a footballer: being strong in your head. This is more than half of the quality you need to be a football player.'

Olivier Giroud

Yet, in some ways, form makes no sense. Why should we place more importance to what happened in the last game than ten matches ago or a hundred matches ago? They are all in the past and they only affect the present and the future if we believe they do.

The majority of footballers, though, take the previous game into the next one. That never creates the consistency that most managers and coaches are looking for. Strikers are a good example of this. If they have a bad run in front of goal when they've been missing chances and not scoring then most will lose confidence. The manager, fans and other players might be talking about it and they start to become tense, doubt themselves and over-think. Some might even start to find ways of avoiding having the chance to score because they fear missing. They pass when they could have shot. They 'hide' on the pitch.

The best strikers, though, don't do that. They maintain confidence and self-belief regardless of

'People in football love to talk about mental strength. Well, I'm the strongest dude you're ever going to meet. Because I remember sitting in the dark with my brother and my mom, saying our prayers, and thinking, believing, knowing ... it's [success] going to happen.'

Romelu Lukaku

what's perceived as their current 'form'. I played with two, Alan Shearer and Billy Sharp, whose mindset was their biggest asset. Their appetite to score goals was insatiable. It was what they lived for. Shearer spoke about how every time he went on the pitch he expected to score. Sharp is the same. And when you play with that kind of confidence and self-belief and trust in yourself, then you play instinctively and the goals just happen.

I developed a process to help me take Shearer and Sharp's mentality into games: 24 hours after a game I would consciously 'press' a re-set button in my head, consigning the game to history. After that, it had no more relevance than all the hundreds of other games I had played previously. That helped me move on to the next game with a consistent belief and confidence.

▌SELF-TALK

Linked to the re-set button are self-image and self-talk.

Looking back it's clear to me that I saw myself as a small-town boy for whom certain things weren't achievable, and thought I lacked the physique to play at the highest level. That created a blockage because it's very unusual (and very difficult) for any of us to outperform what we believe we are capable of. We are who we think we are, therefore we are likely to get the results we think we will.

Our self-image gets reinforced by 'self-talk', by which I mean the 'inner voice' inside our head that for many people annoyingly likes to brood over mistakes, point out what might go wrong and is highly critical. That was totally me and my family (my mum, in particular, is a proper worrier) and I used to go to bed fretting about what people thought of me and all the bad things that had happened and could happen to me. If this inner voice is constantly repeating phrases like 'I can't do this', 'I'm rubbish at this' and 'I'm not good enough' then it's bound to affect your self-perception.

Self-talk can also be the words you use when talking to others. So whenever anybody asked me how I was doing I tended to say 'yeah, not bad' or 'yeah, all right'. Now, I've learned to say 'yeah, I'm really, really good' or 'I'm amazing' so that I'm constantly reinforcing to myself that I'm in a good place. And, sure enough, it helps me to feel better and more positive. Now I never speak negatively to myself. Ever. I'm much more upbeat. I'm thinking and saying phrases like 'I'll be good at this', 'I'm expecting this to go well' and 'I'm going to prove them wrong'.

Often psychological breakthroughs lead to achievement in reality so think about whether you have a self-image that may not allow you to fulfil your full potential. Listen to your inner voice. Everything you say – whether in your head or out loud – has a consequence.

▌VISUALISATION

I'm a huge believer in visualisation and the law of attraction. I've already mentioned how I 'prayed' for a hat-trick the night before the game at Lilleshall during the England under-16 trials, and it came true. Although I had no awareness of what I was doing, this was an early illustration of the power of visualisation.

For a while I didn't tell anyone but because I thought they're just going to laugh at me or won't believe me. Now, I've read about it and realise that the likes of Cristiano Ronaldo and Wayne Rooney – and many other elite performers across all walks of life – have used it throughout their careers. Put simply – and without getting into the technicalities of how the human brain works – if you vividly day-dream or visualise something that you want to happen in advance it becomes more likely to happen in reality. It is also known as the 'law of attraction.' It's that feeling of wanting something so badly that you're almost thinking it into existence. We gravitate towards whatever we focus our attention on.

The textbook way to visualise is quite simple. You sit in a comfortable position, close your eyes and imagine — in as vivid detail as you can — what you would be looking at if the dream you have had already happened. Imagine being inside of yourself, looking out through your eyes at the ideal result.

But different people do it in different ways. When I was younger I used to set goals and then visualise the goals coming true. I used experiences from the past when I felt really good. Nowadays I tend to visualise and pre-plan what I want from the next day and the next week as I'm going to sleep. It's almost like meditation.

It's for each person to find a way that works for them and the concept of visualisation is not a new one, so there's plenty of information out there if people want to do their research. That said, I remember attending a presentation given by the first team psychologist at Liverpool on the benefits of visualisation about ten years ago. Most players didn't take it seriously and acted as though he'd lost his marbles! But by then I had visualised things happening and then those things had come true.

So I'm a big believer. I've been looking into it more and more and realise I attract most of what comes to me.

Billy Sharp also follows the law of attraction but I'm not sure he knows or cares about the science behind it. He talked to me about scoring his first Premier League goal for Sheffield United in his first game. 'I just knew I was going to score if I got on,' he said, and, sure enough, he did.

▍BODY LANGUAGE

Finally, we need to focus on non-verbal communication or, as it's more commonly described, body language. There is evidence that when communicating face to face with people 55 per cent is through body language, 38 per cent through tone and only 7 per cent through the actual words. Of course, body language is a sophisticated subject but here are four key elements:

FACIAL EXPRESSIONS – the human face can express countless emotions. Smiling, for instance, is an incredibly powerful signal to others and an expression of happiness. Indications of sadness, anger, surprise, fear and disgust are the same all around the world.

BODY MOVEMENTS AND POSTURE – the way you move, sit, walk, stand up, hold your head and carry yourself.

GESTURES – we tend to wave, point, beckon and use our hands when we're arguing or speaking animatedly—expressing ourselves without thinking.

EYE CONTACT – since the visual sense is dominant for most people, eye contact is a vital type of nonverbal communication.

It's one thing to 'read' other people (most of us are pretty tuned into that), but quite another to control your body language. Many gestures and signals are unconsciously delivered and it's been described as a language we all speak but few understand.

So, if a footballer is playing in a stadium with, say, 15,000 fans, they won't be able to hear the player but they will be able to see his facial expressions, body movements, posture and gestures. It's no surprise that the players who show positive body language, run around and give 100 per cent every single week become fans' favourites, whereas the ones who throw their arms around, slouch and look like they don't care aren't viewed as favourably.

Craig Bellamy and his assertive
body language. Always looked
confident and up for it.
© Newcastle United Football Club

Equally, if a player receives feedback from a coach or manager and scowls throughout, arms crossed, failing to make eye contact, then you can guess the kind of impression that's going to create.

I picked somebody to copy during training and games and chose Craig Bellamy. I had played with Craig and watched him on the telly and he always looked confident and up for it, like he was ready to run through a brick wall to win. So I mirrored his body language – shoulders back, head up, deep breaths. The change was incredible. It transformed everything that I did on the pitch. To some extent, I also started doing it in training. I changed my reactions so that when I lost the ball I didn't throw my head back in frustration, I focused on getting it back.

Even off the pitch whenever I walk anywhere I'm conscious that I want to look like I'm confident. Head up, chest out. It makes a massive difference – both to how I feel and how I portray myself to others. So I'd say to all footballers: think about your body language. What does it say to others?

▎PREPARATION

Finally, a practical aspect. Recognise that part of match-day confidence comes from having done the necessary preparation work. If you know that you have worked hard in training all week, looked after your body, slept well and done everything you need to do to give yourself the best chance of success on a match-day then that is a great starting point. It will make you feel more assured.

Switch it around the other way: if you've gone through the motions at training all week, over-socialised, stayed up late and switched off during the team talk then that is bound to lead to you feeling underprepared and your confidence levels will suffer.

TAKEAWAYS

■ Form and slumps mainly exist in the mind. Get used to pressing your re-set button and consigning the previous game/experience to the past.

■ Understand and be aware of the power of self-talk, visualisation and body language.

■ Fail to prepare, prepare to fail. It's a cliché, but it's true. Knowing that you've given yourself the best chance of success builds self-belief and confidence.

RESILIENCE AND COURAGE

4

SPRINGBOARD?

■ A NEW ST JAMES' PARK

BY THE AGE of 21, my career had reached a crossroads. Hartlepool were unable to sign me at the end of my second loan spell and my contract at Newcastle United was running down, with little prospect that I was about to break into the senior squad. I could have gone back there and played in the reserves for the last year, hoping that I might be able to change Sir Bobby's mind or, if a new manager took over, hope they saw things differently. However, I felt like I had no time to waste. I wanted first-team football where I could create a reputation and make a difference. So I decided to gamble on a fresh start and worked with my agent to see what was out there.

I went on trial at Northampton, playing against Fulham at Fulham's training ground. I thought I did well, but didn't hear back from them. Then Division Three Exeter City showed an interest. I spoke to their manager, John Cornforth, and the deal was agreed, even though the money was less than ideal. The ITV digital money, which had been a lucrative source of income in the Football League, had just crashed and there was a lot of panic with clubs making cutbacks and offering poor contracts, but at least I'd be playing first-team football; it brought me a change of scenery and, hopefully, a springboard for my career.

In hindsight, now nearly 20 years on, I think signing for Exeter was a bad move. At that time I had an agent who was just starting in football and I became his first-ever client. I put my trust in him – and subsequently he's become well established and had a successful career – but he admitted to me later that he was still learning the ropes when he negotiated that move and can't believe what he did.

Certainly, it would be difficult to think of two clubs that were more different. Coincidentally, both home grounds were called St James' Park but that was the only similarity. Newcastle United in the North East to Exeter City in the South West was a six-hour drive of 366 miles. Few clubs were that far apart geographically. They were also at opposing ends of football's hierarchy. One was a Premier League club, regularly participating in the Champions League, with state-of-the-art facilities and average attendances in 2001/02 of over 51,000. The other was stuck in the lowest tier of English professional football, where they had been struggling forever. The last home game of the previous season had attracted 3,595 fans to a 2-0 defeat to Hartlepool.

My dad believes that the gap in the club's statuses was the main problem with the transfer and that if I have moved down to the Championship or League One it would have worked out better, and he may have had a point. Yet when I signed I was relieved. I knew it was over at Newcastle and I was excited for the new chapter.

URI AND JACKO

Another difference between Exeter and Newcastle was that Exeter had celebrities such as Uri Geller, Michael Jackson, David Blaine and even Darth Vader (or more accurately David Prowse who was the actor) involved with the club! In truth, it was one of the most bizarre set-ups in English football history. Uri had become a famous television personality as a magician, psychic and for his apparent ability to bend spoons just by gently stroking them. A month before I joined the club he'd appeared on *I'm a Celebrity … Get me out of here!*

He was appointed co-chairman of the club in 2002 and his heart was in the right place. He rang me all the time and couldn't have been nicer or more helpful.

He also brought along some of his celebrity friends, with Michael Jackson, arguably the greatest pop icon of all time, joining the Board! Michael had been Uri's best man when he renewed his wedding vows in 2001. I was a big Jacko fan and asked Uri if he could arrange for me to meet him. He did come down to the stadium once and met just about everybody else, though I missed out. It was all a bit surreal and an early indication that although life at Exeter might be interesting, it wasn't the most professional or organised set-up.

BEE'S KNEES

Nevertheless, my new start began well. During preseason in Finland I felt fresh and revitalised and had a bit of a Premier League strut, confident I could stand out at this level. I made my league debut against Shrewsbury Town and, two weeks later, scored my first goal for the club against the local rivals Torquay United with a headline-making volley. I loved it at the start; waking up every morning, making the ten-minute drive to work, enjoying the training, working towards each new game, relishing getting picked every week and playing first-team football.

Then John Cornforth got sacked, two months into the new season. That decision wasn't popular with the fans, or myself. I was convinced that the club had got it wrong and was pretty vocal about it. Perhaps because of that I didn't see eye to eye with the new manager, Neil McNab. I struggled to build a relationship with him and felt him he didn't rate me. My motivation and performances dipped; I wasn't living right, wasn't working hard enough but still had an ego, thought I was the bee's knees and blamed everybody and everything. So he was right to challenge me. I was massively in the wrong and started to get left out of the team.

BAD HABITS

By now I was aware that I had walked into a team and a football club that had been struggling around the bottom of the league for several seasons, and had a deep-rooted losing mentality. Defeats were the norm but we soon forgot about them, going out and drinking after the match. The next day we'd be back in for training, moving on, still going through the motions. The only shock came when we won a game!

I wasn't a good loser, and at first I found this passive acceptance odd but within three or four months I conformed to the culture. I got sucked back into some bad ways of living: drinking, gambling, eating junk food. As a group we were unprofessional, a bit like the reserves at Newcastle. We'd go out binge-drinking on a Saturday night, sometimes Sunday, usually Tuesday, and because there was no food available at the training ground, often have a pub lunch. I moved in with a teammate, Justin Walker, but that didn't help; we spent more time going out than playing football. Certainly, nobody was reigning me in, yet as a headstrong 21-year-old I wouldn't have listened anyway. I thought it was okay because others were doing it as well.

I gambled too. It started when one of the lads and I went into a bookmaker. He only had two-pound coins on him, fed them into the one-armed bandit slot machine and won £90. Seemed easy! We got hooked in and spent an entire afternoon there. We went in the following day too, and it soon became an expensive habit. Two-pound coins progressed to £10, £50, £100 and finally the maximum of £500.

It didn't help that, for the first time, I was alone and hundreds of miles away from my girlfriend and family, far distant from the Guisborough bubble that I loved so much. Despite all the socialising I was homesick and lonely. To his great credit, my dad kept churning out the miles and managed to come to some of the games. I remember once, when we hadn't seen each other for a while and he was going through a tough time with my mum, we met near the team bus at the end of a game and we both got upset and broke down. Although friends and Lucie, my girlfriend (who later became my wife) travelled down when they could it just wasn't the same. Even if I managed to get back up north it didn't have the warm feeling that I enjoyed so much during my childhood. I wasn't quite sure where home was for me anymore.

Besides, Grandad Herbert's death and my mum and dad's divorce were still eating away at me. It was a bad time that was reflected in my standards in training and on a match-day. I was so inconsistent. Sometimes I put in a starring nine-out-of-ten performance but that was followed by a series of five or six-out-of-ten displays. I played 43 league games that year, but Exeter fans didn't see the best of me and as we moved towards the end of the season we faced the threat of relegation out of the Football League.

Managers came and went and in February 2003 Gary Peters took over. He was the opposite of Neil McNab and had faith in me, instructing everyone to 'pass him the ball and he'll win us games'. He probably managed me as well as anyone. In the last four games we drew against Oxford, won away at Swansea and York City and went into the last game against Southend United knowing that a win would keep us up if Swansea got beaten. We scored in the 90th minute to win but Swansea, who had been losing, came back to beat Hull City 4-2. We got relegated to the Conference by a point.

ON THE EDGE

In five years my career had gone full circle – from Non-League up to the Premier League and back again. Little wonder that during the off-season in the summer of 2003 I had a wobble and questioned my future in the game. I knew I'd lost my way. Did I want to be playing Non-League football on the other side of the country to my family? Why was I doing this? What was it all for? My thinking was scrambled. I was in a dark place and miserable.

I spoke to my girlfriend and family. I thought about other career options and nearly walked away from professional football entirely. In the end, only one thing was clear – I didn't want to go back to Exeter and, as a result, failed to turn up for pre-season, which was totally out of character for me but showed how strongly I felt. Of course, my absence didn't go down too well; thankfully, though, the new manager, Eamonn Dolan, took a measured, empathetic approach when he called me.

MAIN MAN

In fact, it's a phone call I'll always remember. I was playing golf when he rang and said, 'I want you to come back. I absolutely love you. I think you've got so much to offer this club. You're our best player, you'll be my main man. Come back, and I'll give you Mondays off so you can travel back home and spend more time with your family. You are a massive part of this team. I can help you.'

I like to think Eamonn saw that I lacked the right kind of support during my first season with the club and that, deep down, I had the work ethic, ambition and ability to be successful. It was just finding a way to get it out of me. At that stage of my career, a supportive manager was so important to my motivation and sense of well-being and he provided the backing I needed to persuade me to stay. He worked wonders to turnaround my thinking.

Eamonn *got* that players are human beings above all else, and treated me that way. Rather than play the disciplinarian or not make the effort at all, he appreciated that I was struggling and that he had to support and help me solve my problems to get the best out of me. I've found that the best managers are flexible enough to treat each player individually. That doesn't mean they are soft or weak, allowing others to take advantage of them; just that they can change their style when they need to. That phone call was a great start.

I remember driving back into Exeter and getting flashed by a speed camera. That felt like a bad omen – like I was continuing the downbeat feeling of the previous season – but Eamonn was true to his word and the season went well. He built the team around me and gave me Mondays off as promised. I repaid his support and trust by lighting up the Conference to such an extent that Doncaster Rovers put in a bid in January 2003. I could have gone but felt loyalty towards Eamonn and said to him, 'Look, I'm happy to stay. You showed faith in me, I'll try and help the team get into the play-offs, and hopefully Doncaster will come back in at the end of the season. If we don't get promoted I'll go then.'

▌'WHAT AM I ACTUALLY DOING?'

During that season in the Conference I was selected to represent England C, which features players who play for clubs outside the Premier League and the English Football League, essentially the best of the best playing Non-League football.

I vividly remember that the whole squad were in a room and, one by one, we were asked to tell everybody our name and a little bit about ourselves. I stood up and said, 'I'm James Coppinger, 22 years old. I made my Premier League debut for Newcastle against Tottenham a couple of years ago. Now I'm playing for Exeter in the Conference.' They couldn't believe it. They said, 'What on earth are you doing here?' Everyone in the room was shocked. It was also a sobering moment for me and I asked myself why and how I'd fallen so far down the ladder. It was my first real moment of self-awareness and it stuck with me.

So when we missed out on the play-offs by one point on the last day of the season it felt like time to move on. My two seasons at Exeter had been psychologically tough but filled with life lessons. I grew up a bit.

As I moved in one direction, Eamonn Dolan went another. After Exeter he became Head of the Academy at Reading, where he achieved great things and I know he was highly thought of. I'll always be grateful for the support and belief he showed towards me. Sadly he lost his life a few years ago. A fantastic manager and human being.

EYEWITNESS

JOHN COPPINGER

My dad has been my longest and most loyal supporter, going to hundreds of games and clocking up thousands of miles. I remember when I played for England under-16s his business was struggling and we played in a tournament at venues such as Rushden and Diamonds, Northampton and Kettering. As they were so far from our home in the North-East – and he couldn't afford bed and breakfast accommodation at the time – he used to sleep in the car. True devotion to duty.

There's no one better placed to assess how my upbringing and character influenced the way I acted in my youth and during the early, rollercoaster stage of my footballing career.

Here are his thoughts:

STRONG-WILLED – 'If he didn't want to do anything James wouldn't do it. That's not to say he was insubordinate, insolent or badly behaved – but he knew his own mind and nothing would move him. I remember James played on the wing at Marton Juniors. Because the ones in the middle were so keen to prove themselves to scouts he wouldn't get the ball and he would completely lose interest and say, "I want to come off" and get subbed.'

SELF-CONSCIOUS – 'As a teenager I would have classed James as deep and very self-conscious. He was introverted. I've got hundreds of photos of James in teams and it struck me that he would always be at the end of the row. When he was at Newcastle the reserves used to play at the Kingston Park Stadium, which is Newcastle Falcons Rugby Ground, and after the matches young kids wanted autographs from anyone who was playing. Whereas some of the lads revelled in going out and being "Billy Big Time", James felt embarrassed and used to sneak around the back to meet me to avoid having to sign.

'I tried to impress upon James where he was, how well he'd done and that he deserved to be there but he never gave me the impression that he felt that he did. One hundred per cent, I think he felt like an imposter at Newcastle – surrounded by the legends like Kenny Dalglish, Ruud Gullit, Bobby Robson, Alan Shearer, John Barnes, Stuart Pearce and Ian Rush – and with England under-16s where it must have been difficult not to feel slightly overawed with Joe Cole doing rabonas all over the field!'

SMALL TOWN MENTALITY – 'I grew up in Guisborough and although Middlesbrough is eight miles down the road it could be a million miles away in terms of how people are and how people act. They are what we call townies. They have an edge to them, almost a swagger. Middlesbrough can be a rough town, whereas Guisborough is a bit more genteel. In Guisborough nobody knew anybody that had been a professional footballer and had been on that journey so it was difficult to imagine that as a career path. It just wasn't something that happened to kids from our area. Other than his best friends Mark Robinson and Greg Booth, his teammates at Marton were from Middlesbrough, and the difference was chalk and cheese. The ones from Middlesbrough oozed confidence they were going to be professional footballers. That's all they wanted to do.'

SUPPORTIVE PARENT – 'Nobody was pushing him and pushing him. All we did was support him. I didn't think I had much choice. If I've been a pushy parent he would have just gone the other way. To me, his happiness was more important than him being a professional footballer. When he did become a pro and went to Newcastle the reason why I didn't get involved is that I had no experience to draw on as nobody I knew had been in my position with a son who was playing professional football. The last thing I wanted to do was make a decision that would cost him his career. By the time he was at Newcastle he was associated with specialists so anything I said would have come across as amateurish. I just stood back and trusted them. I don't think that he would have listened to me anyway.'

WATCHING JAMES PLAY – 'I've tried to be optimistic when going to watch James play but I'm afraid that most of the time I've watched with trepidation (Boro fans will understand that mindset]. I'm more down if he plays badly than high if he plays well. I'm nervous thinking "don't give the ball away in front of the back four, don't let yourself down." If I'm watching him play on the telly and he has a bad game I think "oh god, all those people watching".

'It's a terrible thing because I really should be going with a spring in my step thinking this is going to be great, especially with the kind of player he is. He's the type of player who I would go and watch just because they were playing. Some fans at Exeter told me he's the best player ever to have played for the club. James will do one thing in a match and I think 'I'd have paid money just to see him do that'. I grew up watching entertainers like George Best, Stan Bowles, Rodney Marsh, Frank Worthington and, closer to home, Juninho; players who entertained the crowd. The biggest compliment I can pay him in terms of footballing ability is that he reminds me of those players.'

⌐ANALYSIS⌐

RESILIENCE AND COURAGE

Professional football can be a cut-throat, ruthless business where players are seen as resources and commodities that exist to help the club they represent become more successful.

Life as a footballer would be serene if you always played well and the team always won; if the manager and the fans loved you; if you never got injured and your personal life was permanently filled with love and joy. Truth is, we all know that's never going to happen – for anyone. Every career has challenges and setbacks and every player who has ever played the game – Pele, Maradona and Messi included – has had to deal with them. It goes with the job. Issues constantly bubble up, there are puzzles to solve, and things go wrong.

Some players have faced challenges I've not experienced such as deprived upbringings and career-threatening injuries – but if we use my career as a reasonable example then here's a list, in no particular order, of some of the tests I'd faced – some life-changing, some comparatively trivial – by 24 years old when I was at the end of my time at Exeter:

- Rejected at trials by clubs
- Criticised by managers, coaches, teammates and supporters
- Managers and coaches who didn't rate me
- Getting left out of the team
- Getting sent off and suspended
- Losing
- Playing badly
- Disagreements and conflict with other people
- Changes of clubs, teammates, coaches and managers
- Death of loved ones
- Parents divorcing
- Moving out from home
- Moving from one end of the country to the other, away from my family and friends

In the previous chapters I've touched on some of the ways I dealt with this (all unconsciously as I had very little self-awareness) and they included:

- Taking criticism to heart and losing confidence
- Blaming others and playing the victim
- Allowing relationships to become damaged and unhelpful
- Trying to prove people wrong
- Finding short-term forms of gratification – e.g. socialising and drinking
- Pretending I didn't care

- Avoiding having personal aspirations and ambitions to ensure that I couldn't fail to achieve them
- Sulking and moaning
- Worrying and fretting
- Ignoring advice and guidance from others

It's perfectly normal for anyone in any walk of life to face challenges and setbacks. Every single person on this planet, whether they're sleeping on the streets or a billionaire, has them. Events occur that test us all. The true examination is how we deal with them so that we become more resilient ('the ability to be able to withstand or recover quickly from difficult conditions') and strong-minded.

You can see from my list that with one exception – the desire to prove people wrong – the approaches I took in my early years weren't helping me. Fortunately, as I matured, my mindset evolved and I developed the confidence and courage to try new approaches and became better in coping – as will become apparent during the rest of the book.

Based on that development in the rest of this chapter I share my advice:

FOCUS ON THE TARGET – Firstly, focus on where you want to get to. When you do that then it gives you purpose and drive and when disappointments arise you stand a better chance of realising that they are just a temporary inconvenience that presents an opportunity to learn rather than the

> 'Failure happens all the time. It happens every day in practice. What makes you better is how you react to it.'
>
> Mia Hamm

end of the road. Every challenge and every difficulty you successfully confront will strengthen your will, confidence and ability to deal with future obstacles.

ACCEPT THAT CHALLENGES AND SETBACKS ARE INEVITABLE – Don't be surprised or shocked when challenges and setbacks come along. They are part and parcel of both football and day-to-day life, so put your energies and intellect into developing strategies to deal with them. Prepare yourself mentally for confronting them head-on and relish the challenge. Make the best out of the situation and find a way of dealing with it. See setbacks as a way of learning.

PRESS THE RE-SET BUTTON – As I mentioned previously I developed a principle that I would allow myself 24 hours after a game to reflect and to feel sorry for myself if we got hammered and/or I had a shocker.

Then I pressed the re-set button and moved the memories and emotions associated with the game into the same 'folder' as the other hundreds of games I had played. Essentially that game was forgotten and all my focus was on the future. I lived by that ethos for the last 12 or so years of my career and it stood me in good stead. I also think the concept applies outside of games of football. When you have disappointments don't wallow for too long. Move on and take action.

COURAGE TO CHANGE – On a similar theme don't be resistant to change. Most people have an instinct to avoid or defy it, maybe because they are creatures of habit, fear they lack the competence to change or feel connected to other people who are identified with the old way. My loyalty to John Cornforth, my first manager at Exeter City, was an example of that. It was fine that I was disappointed that he lost his job, but unacceptable that I allowed that disappointment to sour my relationship with the next manager and influence my performances on the pitch. Learn to accept change, make it work for you and, better still, take the initiative to create the changes you want.

BE TOLERANT AND HUMBLE – Footballers are constantly receiving feedback and criticism – from managers, coaches, other players, supporters at the match, in the media and on social media. One of the most testing aspects of being a high-profile professional footballer in the modern era is the amount of scrutiny that you come under, with the glare of the spotlight magnified compared to the norm. So how it's dealt with is crucial.

It's a kind of self-protection to be defensive and dismissive of criticism and when that comes from people you work with it can lead to conflict. People or groups of people have fallen out with each other at most clubs I've played for, although it often bubbles away beneath the surface with the gossip, rumour and back-biting done in the shadows. Mick Wadsworth and Neil McNab are two of the people I fell out with during my early career when I lacked the maturity to deal with their feedback. At that stage, I always thought I was in the right and held grudges. I now know it's okay to be wrong and okay to admit you were wrong to others.

Listen to feedback and respect options and views, even if you disagree with them and disregard them.

BE FLEXIBLE – Some people always deal with conflict the same way. At one extreme they may always take a firm stance, fighting for what they want; at the other they may avoid conflicts entirely, keen not to hurt feelings or damage relationships. My advice is to be flexible in how you address each situation. One size doesn't fit all. Sometimes it may be best to 'compete', sometimes it may be best to 'avoid'. Choose your battles, depending on the issue, the importance and the person.

USE CRITICISM AS A SOURCE OF MOTIVATION – This is one of the traits that I found easy. I've always remembered people who doubted me, whether it was the teacher at school who picked the bigger boy for the county team when it should have been me or Hoggy at Newcastle. I've always been motivated by the challenge of proving people wrong and proving that I can do what I say I'm going to do. I don't know where that instinct comes from, but, of course, it's not just me. Managers try to create a siege mentality where their team feels like the world is against them because they know that it can enhance performance.

HELP YOURSELF AND GET HELP – Be self-aware enough to know when you need support from friends, mentors and specialists and make good use of their time. As will become apparent from my own story, sometimes talking and getting things off your chest can be a massive release. The adage of 'a problem shared is a problem halved' still holds true. Baring your soul is a sign of strength, not weakness.

That's one way of looking after yourself and your sense of well-being – and there are many other ways,

'People point towards the need to handle disappointments when they come along, but you've also got to be able to handle the good things. It's very easy when things are going well to think you're complete. You're never complete.

When you have success it's fantastic but it brings its challenges and it's important to handle it correctly. You don't want to throw it away.'

Sir Kenny Dalglish

ranging from physical exercise, laughter, reading a good book, yoga and meditation. Also, there are stories of people who have overcome immense challenges and insurmountable odds, so draw on their inspiration. It's whatever works for you.

TAKE RESPONSIBILITY – Finally, avoid playing the blame game or looking for scapegoats when things go wrong. That's easy and unproductive. Instead, take responsibility, try to get it right next time and bounce back. This is a massive aspect of a pro mindset, so massive that it has its own chapter and, as a result, I'll only mention it in passing here.

Of course, it's up to each person to find the best way to deal with their challenges. The key point is that it is impossible to sustain a career in professional football if you can't deal with change, conflict and criticism. It goes with the job.

Finally, just to support the comments made by Sir Kenny Dalglish in the foreword to this book. Whilst it's easy to focus on the negatives we can also be derailed by success. Some let it go to their head and lose sight of what created success in the first place. There is a kind of resilience required to avoid falling into that trap.

TAKEAWAYS

■ Everyone has challenges and setbacks – it's part of life. It's how you deal with them that defines your success.

■ Focus on your goals and view setbacks as part of learning and a temporary inconvenience along the journey.

■ Find a way to use feedback to your advantage.

SELF-AWARENESS AND ACCOUNTABILITY

5

FALSE START

HAVING FULFILLED MY promise to Eamonn Dolan, I was delighted that in the summer of 2004 Doncaster Rovers continued the interest they had shown in me during the January transfer window. I went to meet them to discuss a deal.

PORTACABINS AND A BUZZ

The chairman, John Ryan, showed me around the training ground and then took me to the run-down Belle Vue Stadium where the executive boxes were orange portacabins. Yet the pitch was good and there was no doubt that the club was on the up. They had just celebrated back-to-back promotions: from the Conference into League Two and then League Two into League One. There was a real buzz about the place, and much of that came from their larger-than-life chairman. He lived and breathed the club like a superfan, knew everything about it and was positively bursting with energy, optimism and enthusiasm. He talked about Doncaster making it to the Championship, Doncaster moving to a new stadium, Doncaster doing this, Doncaster doing this.

I thought 'Who is this guy? What is he on about? Has he lost the plot?' Yet he undeniably had charisma and drive. The more I got to know him, the more I understood how he had been successful in his business life.

I loved that they were offering me the opportunity to get back on track, rebuild my football career back up north where I believed I belonged, with my family close by and at an ambitious club. So in May 2004 I signed for Doncaster and the compensation fee was around £30,000. It would be an understatement to suggest that the deal worked out well for both parties; though it didn't look like that in the beginning ...

▍OVERTHINKING

When I signed I was interested to find out why the club had climbed up the leagues. The manager, Dave Penney, was quick to tell me how hard they worked and it was evident from the first day of pre-season that they also had team spirit and quality, with players such as Michael McIndoe, Paul Green, and Ricky Ravenhill who were perfect for that level and keen to progress their careers.

I missed the first three games through suspension (having been sent off in my last game for Exeter) and that set the tone for my first season in South Yorkshire. On the plus side I did make 38 league and cup appearances but I didn't do myself justice and failed to score. Nothing clicked on the pitch, or off it.

In hindsight, there was a hangover from my struggles at Exeter. I lived alone in a two-bedroom flat at Lakeside and after training I'd come home and spend too much time worrying, fretting and over-thinking. Particularly when I first signed I became isolated and introspective.

Looking back I let others affect and control me – such as the assistant manager who constantly made comments that wound me up – and I didn't take responsibility for my actions. I blamed and became conditioned by other people. I struggled with my self-image and my self-talk; I feared failing and I feared success.

Above all, I feared dying. That went back to my grandad's passing away and, around the same time, my auntie's husband committing suicide. I kept it bottled up but the thought that at any point, I could die, or my mum, dad or sister could die, became a heavy burden to bear. An indication of how this preyed on my mind is the fact that I wrote letters to each of them telling them how much I loved them. In the end, I didn't send them but the sentiments were heartfelt.

By the time the 2005/06 campaign was underway, I was struggling to get picked. The manager Dave Penney was juggling the team to find a formation that worked. There was talk that I might move to local-rivals Rotherham United, who had just been relegated out of the Championship. Fortunately, the manager opted against the switch, I believe partly because he saw glimpses of potential in training where I was more carefree and played as though I was with my mates down the park in Guisborough. I felt comfortable in that environment and the football just flowed. Yet on a match-day, it was as though I was carrying lead weights on my back. I was constantly thinking about the crowd, about the opposition, about the manager – and their view of me – and couldn't repeat my training ground performances. I entered a state of self-doubt where I was frozen with fear; trying way too hard, overthinking and tense.

I found that incredibly frustrating but it's quite a well-known concept in football and sport as a whole. There have been many players who gained a reputation for turning it on during training but not on a match-day. That's not a good reputation to have but, despite the best of intentions, I deserved to be labelled that way at the time.

GUINEA PIG

Fortunately, Dave Penney had been contacted by a behaviourist called Terry Gormley, a specialist in helping people with their mindset. They agreed to meet and Dave, who was pretty old school, told Terry he had all of ten minutes to prove to him that this worked! Terry picked up his bag and said, 'Right I'll see you later then' before adding 'you called me to come in and now you're telling me I've only got ten minutes to tell you if it works!' And that's how it started. Terry suggested: 'Look, if you can give me one player to work with and you can see the results, then it'll give you a better understanding of what this is about.'

Dave had someone in mind. He said, 'We've got a lad called James Coppinger, who is the best player in training by a country mile, but he's not the same on a

Saturday. We can't get what we want out of him. If you can speak to him and make him a better player then it will prove to me that you can achieve something and I'll buy into what you're doing.'

So I became a guinea pig …

LIFE-CHANGER

My life changed on Wednesday, 21 September 2005. It's probably not too dramatic to state that you could split it between the 24 years, eight months, two days and ten hours before I entered the boardroom at Doncaster Rovers' Belle Vue Stadium for my first meeting with Terry Gormley, and everything that has happened since.

OUT OF BODY EXPERIENCE

I entered the boardroom not knowing what to expect but with an open mind. Certainly, the timing was perfect because I knew I was struggling and my career was stagnating. It was worth trying anything to get rid of the dark clouds that hovered above me. I was ready to give it a good go, which was a great starting point.

Terry has told me that many players who come to him don't *really* want to be helped. They go for the sake of it, to tick a box. Footballers can be cynical and guarded about 'Mumbo-jumbo that fills their head with rubbish'. I'm not sure if Terry would have been able to build the trust and rapport with me so quickly when I was younger and at Newcastle, though I suspect he would have got there in the end because he was so skilled at building the relationship and encouraging me to open up and talk. You've got to want to buy into it, and I went all in, almost from the first few seconds.

He asked me about myself and how I had got to this point in my life. So I talked him through my story so far: Darlington, Newcastle, living away from home, getting relegated with Exeter, Mum and Dad's divorce, grandad's death etc. In truth, I hadn't opened up about this kind of stuff to many, if any, people and he saw that some elements of the story – about my grandad for example – caused an instant emotional reaction. I was beginning to get upset.

He asked me to get up from the boardroom chair where I was sitting, stand up, take a few steps away and then look back at myself in the chair as though I was still in it; a kind of out of body experience. He asked, 'What do you see?' and followed up with more questions about this 24-year-old footballer, James Coppinger, sitting there in the chair. 'How would his grandad feel about James?' Of course, that touched more raw nerves. 'How is James feeling?' I told him that James was very sad, lonely, and lacking in confidence. In short, somebody who was struggling.

I found the exercise, which is frequently used in mentoring, therapy and counselling sessions to help view issues from a fresh perspective, absolutely mind-blowing. For probably the first time I looked at myself with clarity, detachment and fresh eyes. The realisation of where I was at in my life hit home.

I'd hardly known Terry for more than 20 minutes and yet the floodgates had been opened. I must have

With Terry Gormley. He transformed my life and we've become firm friends as well as business partners.

© Terry Gormley

been in a dark place psychologically for him to have that much of an influence on me so quickly.

Mental health is a huge issue these days but it wasn't talked about so much then. Since that day if I'm feeling anxious, struggling to cope or worried about something I always speak openly to someone to get things off my chest and re-gain my perspective. The number of people who've committed suicide when they had the world at their feet is scary. It's all about what's in your head and how you process everything, so opening up can be crucial to ease the pressure.

▌LIGHT BULB

Terry explained that the way I was thinking was influencing my football and my whole life. He outlined how the brain works and how it all joins up: my thoughts dictate how I feel, how I feel dictates how I act, and how I act dictates my results. Up until then little of that was working in my favour because of unhelpful thinking habits. My achievements so far were *despite* rather than *because* of my mindset. However, the good news was that I had the potential and capability to choose to change the way I thought so that it could help me.

That was a massive realisation, a light bulb moment. People just tended to say 'that's the way you are' or 'you've been brought up like that'. I thought that, good or bad, I was stuck with my personality and my behaviour. But Terry educated me to understand that was wrong. I had the potential to change my mind-map, the way I thought, and become a new, improved version of myself if I wanted to. It was all about thinking differently and starting to put helpful habits into place.

I thought: 'Right, so all I have to do is think differently to get different results?' and from that moment I started developing what I call a 'professional mindset', something that allowed me to dramatically improve my results.

∎ 'WOW!'

In 90 minutes with Terry I'd gone from thinking 'what is this all about?' to looking back in dismay at how I'd got in the way of my progress. I'm sure if someone had videoed that first session they would have noticed that by the end I had changed. I had a smile on my face, was walking taller and felt hugely energised.

I remember just thinking 'wow'. It seems over the top to say it, but it was honestly life-changing for me.

No one can imagine what a release it was; the biggest weight had been lifted from my shoulders. I remember going home to Lucie, who was to become my wife, and sitting on the top of the kitchen worktop and saying, 'You will never, ever believe what's just happened. Things have just changed!' It was that quick. I could see light at the end of the tunnel. I decided that 'I wasn't having it anymore, I'm gonna take responsibility for my life, and it starts now.'

Fortunately, Lucie was supportive of something that she might have seen as a fad or nonsense. I know other people who have gone through a similar transition and their partner didn't buy into it in the same way. It must have been disorientating for her because I almost changed overnight, albeit for the better. I became more understanding, more self-aware of my role and responsibilities as a partner and, later, as a husband.

#TeamCoppinger. With Lucie and the children. My family has given me the stability and happy home environment that I craved.
© Doncaster Rovers Football Club

I became more much focused and we agreed on goals that defined what we wanted to achieve.

During my time at Exeter, Lucie had been studying at Teesside University – we could hardly have been further away – but we were able to buy a home in Doncaster, get married and create the stability and happy home environment that I craved. To add to that we always wanted kids and Lucie, a paediatric nurse, is maternal and brilliant with children. Over time Finley, Isaac and Phoebe came along, and we also added two dogs to the growing family.

This settling down in a happy home has been my bedrock. As most people will tell you marriage and children take you into a phase of your life where your focus changes and you re-evaluate everything. We've just gone from strength to strength and Lucie's support is a huge part of my footballing achievements. I wouldn't have been able to do it without her and it would be easy to overlook how crucial her buy-in to Terry's guidance was.

▌PUTTING IT INTO PRACTICE

Coincidentally, I had an opportunity to put my learning into practice later on the same day as my first meeting with Terry. I had just come back into Doncaster's starting 11 and rewarded Dave Penney's faith in me with a couple of assists against Scunthorpe, earning a start in the high-profile Carling Cup match against Manchester City. They weren't quite the City of the modern era but they still had England internationals David James in goal, Darius Vassell upfront and were managed by Stuart Pearce.

One of the reasons that Dave wanted me to see Terry was that I'd never scored for Doncaster and it had become a mental block. I was tensing up at the sight of goal, missing when I should score. In the boardroom that morning we went through a visualisation routine about scoring a penalty. I had visualised David James in goal, me stepping up, taking deep breaths, putting the ball on the spot, walking back, picking a corner, then running up and tucking it away, feeling the buzz.

The game was goalless after 90 minutes and went to extra time, where Vassell gave City the lead before a Michael McIndoe penalty saw us back level with two minutes to go. The match went to penalties! Some – including the manager – might have been surprised that I put my hand up to take one of them. Some will have feared the worst! But the visualisation played out in reality. I took Doncaster's second penalty, walked up, put the ball down and sent James the wrong way. What a feeling! Doncaster won the shootout 3-0

On this red-letter day it was Terry's 40th birthday and as he travelled home from his party the first thing he wanted to know was how I had done in the game. He was ecstatic that I'd scored such a decisive penalty, and it continued a Carling Cup run where we also beat Aston Villa before taking on an Arsenal team with Aleksandr Hleb, Gilberto Silva and Robin van Persie. Gilberto had to score a 120th-minute equaliser before Arsenal won the shoot-out. It was those nights when the atmosphere at Belle Vue was unbelievable that helped me to develop self-belief.

POLISHING THE DIAMOND

Of course, there wasn't just one session with Terry. That was just the beginning. Subsequently, we met every week, then every fortnight and then every month. I now knew that the only person who could change me was me, but it was achievable and I was motivated to do it. I was a sponge, soaking it all in, building up my understanding.

Terry used a metaphor that I liked. He talked about how we are all diamonds that become covered in layers of dirt. Negative events and psychological baggage that we carry around obscures the diamond. It can't shine. But as you start dealing with longstanding issues and change the way you think then the dirt begins to become removed, more of the diamond is revealed and it starts to sparkle, getting brighter and brighter until you need to squint or wear sunglasses to even look at it. I could relate to that metaphor and, with his help, worked on getting rid of the dirt.

I became much more accountable for my actions. When people used to say 'are you coming out for a drink?' I had always felt like I had to say 'yes'. Now, when the invite came I'd say 'no thanks, I don't want to'. At first, I'd get a little bit of stick but that soon started to fade away. The people that went out wouldn't ask me anymore and I could get on and do my thing.

If people said I was useless as a footballer I used to believe them. After my sessions with Terry, when managers, coaches, teammates, supporters hammered me I'd filter out the rubbish. The improvement in my sense of well-being and my performances on the pitch was unbelievable. I couldn't believe how easy things were to change. I was blown away.

▌COMFORTABLE IN MY OWN SKIN

As I continued to work with Terry over the months and years the benefits kept stacking up. Without a doubt, I became more socially aware, whether communicating and meeting with a group or with individuals. I used to struggle with that because of my lack of confidence but I learned to just be real and genuine and no longer care what people thought. If they didn't like me it was up to them. I became happy with who I was and comfortable in my own skin.

On the pitch I improved enormously: more assists, more goals, didn't shirk out of anything, didn't let fans, managers, coaches, players affect me. There would be supporters at Exeter who would struggle to believe I'm the same person and no one who watched my first season at Doncaster would have predicted that I would have still been there in 2021 having played more than 600 games, won three promotions and been awarded personal accolades.

Aside from football there are other achievements – trekking for seven days to Machu Picchu in Peru and building my own house to name but two – that can also be traced back to this meeting. I'm a huge convert and it certainly transformed my life.

▌CATALYST

Of course, we all hope to mature and become wiser with age and experience anyway, but Terry's mentoring was the catalyst I needed, and those early sessions were just the start of a lifelong process. Driven by a new-found willingness to improve myself I started taking small steps every day; coming out of my comfort zone, trying new things. It's been a long road but I have relished the opportunity to improve myself as a football player, person, father and husband.

My belief in this philosophy and principles gave me a foundation that I could live my life by. I've stuck to them ever since, not least because as my results improved on and off the pitch I built up complete trust and conviction that they would help me.

In the modern world people want immediate results and instant gratification. This has been a slow-burner and a long journey but the 2021 version of me bears very little resemblance to the 2005 version. I have become more able to turn what others would call negatives into positives and deal with adversity. In my mind, there's not one thing that has happened to me negatively since that day. Other people may perceive that I've had setbacks, problems and bad days, but I've grown into the habit of focusing on only what I can do to put it right or make it better. After a disappointment I always go back to what I've learned and say, 'This is what I tried to do. It's the right thing. Reset and go again.'

Studies indicate we have 60 to 80,000 thoughts per day and I realised the way I controlled and managed them was massively important. In short, I learned that the happiness of my life depends on the quality of my thoughts.

And I'm not the only one who has seen the light. Terry's progress with me was the validation that Dave Penney was looking for and he also worked successfully with three or four other players, particularly Sean McDaid. Sean sadly had to retire through a knee injury in 2011 but was better able to cope with that disappointment because of the work they had done. Sean is now my agent as well as my friend and he is just as enthusiastic as me in promoting the benefits.

EYEWITNESS

TERRY GORMLEY

Terry is someone who wears many hats in business: behaviourist (also known as 'The Mindshaper'), senior partner, business investor, award-winning entrepreneur, coach and mentor. To me, he's simply the person who helped me transform my life by sharing his knowledge. We've become firm friends as well as business partners and he is the first person I would go to if I needed help or some wise words.

FIRST MEETING – 'James was the first person I worked with in football. We met at Belle Vue in the boardroom which was like a small, niche pub with bar stools. He didn't really know why he was there but we soon had a connection that will last a lifetime.

'In the opening minutes I consciously tried to build a rapport with James, picking up and mirroring his use of words, breathing, body language, tone and pace, but James was so open and it was because of him that we were quickly able to build trust. I always think the mind is like a parachute – it has to be open to work. James said, 'Okay tell me what I need to do,' and it was clear that he wanted to make changes and try things. He grasped it and knew it was one ingredient that was part of a successful recipe. That kind of attitude is massively helpful. If his mind had been closed it would have been much more difficult to help him.'

DEVELOPING MINDSET – 'I believe there's an inside world and an outside world. A lot of people, including James at the time, allow the outside world to control their inside world. I always say 'success is an inside job'. It doesn't matter what's going on in the environment around you, it's what's going on inside your head that makes the real difference and James now thinks differently. He was always a super footballer but where he's shone in recent years is developing a strong mind-set. He's become great at the inside game.'

CONFLICT – 'His manager, Dave Penney, told me that if he blasted James in the dressing room it would demotivate him. He also told me that when someone bullied James on the pitch he ended up taking him off because he went into his shell. So I was delighted to watch James grow in confidence and become more forceful.

'I remember against Barnsley, several weeks after we'd started working together, someone smashed him up in the air and over a barrier at the side of the pitch – and he came back, dusted himself off, fronted up and pushed the player. It was the first time he had really stood up for himself mentally, and I watched it on TV and was really proud because I saw that as a big step forward. I've watched him over the years and he doesn't accept being bumped and pushed around anymore.'

STIGMA – 'Everyone thinks things are rubbish until they become the norm. The feeling back in the day was that footballers didn't need to focus on the mental side. They just got on with it. I remember when the England manager, Glenn Hoddle, brought in someone who was described as a faith-healer, and was stigmatised by it because people thought it was weird. It was simply because the managers of the day didn't have any focus on psychological performance when they were players.

'Slowly, though, people in football, are looking for those one per cent marginal gains and understanding the importance of the mental side. Managers of the future may have experience of this as a player and gradually it will become the norm. For instance, if Copps ever becomes a manager – though I don't think he currently intends to go down that route – then I'm sure that he will focus on this area. When you have people like him, who have had better careers than they would have had by employing a pro mindset, then it will seep into the culture. Until that happens, football will continue to be behind other sports.

'I believe that in one hundred years mindset and behaviour will be part of learning and teaching at every school.'

PENALTIES – 'Over the last 30, 40 years the English national football team has traditionally been rubbish at penalties. If you watched the body language, how they were breathing as they stepped up to take the penalties, then you knew that they were nervous and unlikely to do well. This is because they were focusing on negatives and what they didn't want to happen. The mind doesn't do negation and can't tell the difference between *wanting* something to happen and *not wanting* something to happen. Either way, it gravitates towards whatever the mind focuses on, in this case not missing the penalty!

'Compare that to Portugal's Cristiano Ronaldo. He took the penalty to knock England out of the 2006 World Cup quarter final and he did 'keepy-uppys' all the way down to take the kick. His breathed deeply and his body language was positive and powerful. He knew where he was going to hit it and scored. That was all about his strong mentality. He scored primarily because he knew he would.'

PRIDE – 'I'm incredibly proud of the young man that James has turned into. I've watched every step of his career and his behaviour. He's totally responsible for his success. I was just an ingredient in the recipe that he needed in his early days. Over the years I've watched him give so much to others and ask for nothing in return.'

ANALYSIS

SELF-AWARENESS AND ACCOUNTABILITY

There were many gems in Terry Gormley's guidance and the biggest bombshell for me can be summarised in one sentence: the way we think affects the results we achieve, and we can all change the way we think.

I spent the first 24 years of my life with a different view but Terry's education changed everything for me because I was then able to look back at myself and analyse how my thinking patterns, the unique mind-map that I had developed, was having a negative effect.

I realised that my mind could be my friend or my enemy and I had the power to decide.

▮ SELF-AWARENESS

That kind of revelation instantly encouraged me to become more self-aware, so let's start there in working through seven key lessons – all of which link together – from my work with Terry.

No doubt footballers who want to master the mental game need to be able to self-reflect and self-analyse as I did in that 'out-of-body' exercise in the boardroom at Belle Vue when I looked at myself analytically for the first time and began to evaluate where I was and what I wanted to change.

Perhaps understandably, most young footballers are poor at that. They don't pause to analyse, and even if they do, are biased or plain wrong in their thinking. That's why I would say to them that it's important to get feedback from trusted and respected judges who know the game. They will give you priceless information if you are willing to listen. Don't let your ego or insecurities get in the way of going to them for help.

If you do that the result can be a helpful cycle where you play the game, review your performance, learn any lessons and then make changes to keep improving. All the best sportsmen and women do that, and it was an area where Terry helped me make a massive leap forward ...

GOAL-SETTING

... another was becoming clearer in what I wanted out of my footballing career and my life as a whole.

Goal-setting will help you to focus on what's important and give you purpose and direction. It may be a good idea to write the goals down because it makes them feel more real and tangible and, according to studies, increases the likelihood of actually achieving them.

Your goals should be SMART:

S – SPECIFIC

M – MEASURABLE

A – ACHIEVABLE

R – REALISTIC

T – TIME-BASED

That will help you to be crystal clear on what you're trying to achieve, helping your brain and conscious and subconscious thinking to start work in getting you there.

Also, your goals *must* be personalised and meaningful. Whether that's scoring ten goals a season, signing a new pro contract or, away from football, buying a new car you need to be motivated to succeed so that you feel a buzz and a deep sense of achievement when it can be ticked off the list.

Monitor your progress, share it with someone you trust and re-set your goals if your priorities change.

▌ACCOUNTABILITY

The third of Terry's takeaways was the importance of taking responsibility. I had allowed others to make decisions for me that affected my future. It seems so silly but it was only with Terry's help that it hit home that I was letting people walk all over me and take advantage. From that moment I vowed to make all the decisions myself and regained control of my life.

I also realised just how unhelpful it is to play the victim. I'm sure we've all been

> 'Say this to yourself: I am not a victim. I am not a victim in football or in life.'
>
> **Mauricio Pochettino**

guilty of that; I certainly was as has already been documented in this book.

'In football, the worst things are excuses. Excuses mean you cannot grow or move forward.'

Pep Guardiola

Of course, since we are human, it's easy to get caught up in self-pity, 'unfairness of life' and 'why me?' traps; easy to hold our own 'pity party' when we wallow in misery at all the bad luck that life has thrown our way. In our heads it's never our fault and so we find someone or something else to blame. That's an easy habit to get into, not least because it means that we don't have to take responsibility for putting things right. Ultimately, of course, it's self-defeating and unproductive.

I do a lot of work with academy youngsters nowadays and accountability is a topic that I go on and on about. Up until the age of 16 they are not legally accountable for their actions anyway, and nine times out of ten parents will have made most of the decisions for them. They can become closeted and protected.

So leaving school and playing football full time can be a shock. Suddenly they are exposed in a highly competitive, make-or-break environment where the choices they make will go a long way to determining whether they get to sustain a career as a pro. That can be mind-blowing and lonely for some who can't deal with the fact that it's now down to them to work out what's required and take action. The penny drops for some but not others.

Nor is it just youngsters who struggle. I've also played with hundreds of players who've 'made it' but still love to moan and play the victim rather than take responsibility for their actions. Once I was aware of this concept I started noticing just how prevalent it is.

■ CONTROL THE CONTROLLABLES

Linked to 'accountability' Terry kept using a phrase that stuck with me: 'control the controllables', which involves accepting what's outside of your influence and focusing on what you can actually do something about. It's easy for a pro footballer to focus on:

- Training away from the first team
- Not playing as many games as they would like
- The frustration of being injured

Yet their energies are best deployed elsewhere on:

- How they can make themselves and the team better
- What they need to do to improve their performance – technical, tactical, physical, mental
- Doing their injury rehabilitation as thoroughly as possible

Recently someone moaned to me about his manager picking him once every five to ten games and then leaving him out again. He said if they kept on doing that then how could he be expected to play well? In his mind the manager was the problem but I disagreed.

I explained that it was his responsibility to perform brilliantly on the training ground and to impress so much that the manager *wanted* to play him more often. As Sir

Kenny Dalglish said in his foreword managers want the player to be every bit as successful as they want to be themselves, so my advice was to speak with the boss, listen, find out what he needs from you to help him pick you more often and then give it 100 per cent every day in training.

Even if those managerial decisions were purely tactical then I suggested that it was down to the player to recognise that they weren't currently the right fit in the formation and do everything they could to encourage the manager to change his approach. If they did all that and the manager explained 'you're doing everything right, your attitude is great, but you're just not the kind of player I want' then at least the player would know and could have a conversation about going on loan or getting a transfer. I suppose the key point is that a player can't control the manager's actions but he can control his own. Whinging and sulking isn't going to work; taking responsibility might.

In short, it's important to focus on what's within your control. You only have a certain amount of energy so why waste it in areas that you can't directly affect?

▍RE-FRAMING

The fifth technique that Terry shared with me was to re-frame how I thought about events. I was encouraged to adopt the approach that was going to lead to the best outcomes for me, rather than simply being led by my emotions. I learned that it wasn't the event so much as the way I thought about it that dictated my happiness and sense of well-being.

An example of this was the way I dealt with losing loved ones. As I've explained before in the book, I found bereavement and grieving to be a psychological problem that continued long, long after the loss. However, with support, I came to realise that it would be helpful if I thought about the subject differently and that doing so wasn't disrespectful to the people I lost.

Sadly, in my mid-30s, in fairly quick succession I lost my nan, grandad (Coppinger), grandma and mother-in-law, who suffered a brain tumour. In three of those instances, I was there with them when they passed away and watching them deteriorate and take their last breath was, of course, incredibly tough to take.

However, armed with greater maturity and a stronger, more resilient mindset I chose to celebrate their lives, take inspiration from all they had achieved and remember the good times we had together. As you'll find in a forthcoming chapter Grandad Coppinger's death became the catalyst for an outstanding season, which was a positive way to honour his memory.

On a similar theme, I became aware that I was spending a lot of time worrying about events that may not happen. My parents and my nana were worriers and they conditioned my thinking to some extent. However, I realised, with Terry's help, how I was feeding my brain with unhelpful negative thoughts: 'I hope I don't play badly', 'I hope I don't miss when a chance to score comes my way' etc. etc. That achieved nothing and, worse, because of the way the brain works it made the event I didn't want to happen more likely!

So I'd suggest thinking about your thinking! Is the way you view events and situations always helpful or could they be re-framed in a more positive direction?

▌MASSIVE ACTION

Of course, all those tools, techniques and theories are just words unless you put them in practice! Talk is cheap! You have to act!

When I'm speaking to players I use the analogy of baking a cake. If it doesn't taste good then you would change the ingredients. If you have the potential to improve at an aspect then why would you keep doing the same thing over and over again and expect different results? It just doesn't make sense to me. It's the definition of insanity to keep doing the same things yet expect a different result, so you've got to change how you look at things and change how you think.

You have to start somewhere. These are all just habits. So if your inner voice tells you that it's difficult to start doing things differently then replace it with a more positive approach: 'I can do it', and 'I will do it'. Change the way you speak to yourself. Eventually, new habits will be formed and you won't be able to (and won't want to) go back to how you were.

I think personal development and mental health are a daily battle for every single person yet many go through life hoping things will change for the better but not doing anything that might make it happen.

Even if you try to make changes you still need the drive and discipline to stick at it. If I tried something and it didn't immediately work out then I used to give up and mark it down as a failure. I learned that I needed to be brave enough to keep trying and, sometimes, keep failing. If it didn't work out, try it again but in a different way. Just keep trying, keep trying, keep trying until I got there.

Terry used the analogy that everyone at school knew a girl they wanted to ask out – but didn't do so because they were too scared of rejection. They didn't want the risk of getting a 'no'. Terry's viewpoint was that they 'already had the no' by not asking her out so, in a sense, there was nothing to lose.

Terry soon sussed me out as someone who was analytical, might think too much and become paralysed considering the pros and cons of trying something new. Terry cut through all of that. He said to me, 'Just do it. What's the worst that can happen? That it doesn't work out for you? Well, that's where you are already!' It took me a while to remove the shackles, but my philosophy moved on from *overthinking* to *just do it*. Every time I see the Nike slogan it reminds me!

▌COMFORT ZONE

Of course to do that you might need to step out of your comfort zone. Most people decline to do so, even if, deep down, they know it might not be the best place for them to be.

Another one of Terry's analogies involves thinking of a hula-hoop. If you put it over your head and let it drop to the floor then everything you experience in your life at that moment is inside the circle (your comfort zone): your current state of health, your fitness, your style of parenting, your friendships, your current job, your finances, and so much more.

Everything that you desire in life but do not currently have is outside of the hula-hoop and to move it inside you will probably need to do something that makes you feel disorientated and uncomfortable.

High performers in all walks of life do this all the time to try and get better. They're not afraid to put themselves out of their comfort zone

In summary, it feels to me like the text in this chapter should be in bold and underlined! If you can understand and implement Terry's takeaways then it can only help you master the mental game. And if you haven't yet appreciated how important I think that is to success in football – and life – then you haven't been paying attention!

> 'I try to get better in every aspect of my life, not just on the football field. I am competitive and I just always want to get better.'
>
> Raheem Sterling

TAKEAWAYS

- Become self-aware and become responsible for your own decisions and actions. It's your life: don't play the victim or let others dictate to you.
- Write down your goals and make them SMART.
- Take massive action! Be brave, get out of your comfort zone and just do it!

TEAMWORK AND

6 CONSISTENCY

PRIME TIME

TERRY GORMLEY'S INVOLVEMENT heralded my best season so far in professional football with 43 league and cup appearances and five goals. I became one of the first names on the Doncaster team sheet, our run in the Carling Cup promised much for the future and in winning our last four games we only just missed out on the League One play-offs, eventually finishing eighth. My performances attracted Championship clubs to show an interest in buying me, although I was unaware at the time and the club turned away any offers.

We started the 2006/07 season with optimism so it came as a surprise when, at the end of August, manager, Dave Penney left the club by 'mutual consent.' Having spent eight years with the club, as player and manager, it was agreed a change was necessary for both parties.

Soon after, John Ryan appointed Bournemouth manager Sean O'Driscoll as manager, with Richard O'Kelly as his assistant. This proved to be a masterstroke. Dave moved us up the leagues; now Sean and Richard took us to new levels over a five-year period that was the most successful in the club's history. Doncaster had never reached the Championship before but during Sean's tenure we not only gained promotion to it but stayed there. At one stage there was even the outside possibility of reaching the Premier League. There is an unwritten hierarchy based on each club's facilities, resources and finances and during this period Doncaster undoubtedly overachieved.

EAGLE EYE

I had a meeting with the new management team on their first day. I must confess that I didn't know who was who at the time, and I assumed that the more vocal, dominant and louder one was the new 'gaffer'. Then we went out to train and I found I'd been wrong. Richard, the assistant, was bursting with bubbly encouragement, whereas Sean, the manager, was low key. Apparently, he had earned the ironic name of 'noisy' when he was a player and didn't use ten words when three could convey the same message. It was a sign of confidence and strength that he didn't feel the need to assert his authority and establish credibility by shouting at his new set of footballers to show he was in charge.

That soon became clear anyway and we realised that Sean was a one-off. He watched and listened and had an eagle eye for details. He was always tuned in to stuff that other managers overlooked: my movement on and off the ball, how focused I was in training, how I applied myself from day to day, my love for football, the way I tried to affect others. He was all-seeing!

For training we all had to wear long socks with shin pads, we did warm-ups where he was constantly testing our brains, then we'd do passing drills and scenario-based game sessions with uneven numbers or with multiple restrictions and conditions. It tested you mentally, and a bit like Alan Irvine, my youth team manager at Newcastle, Sean set and enforced high standards.

It was complicated at times and he did things very differently so he needed everyone's buy-in for it to work. His approach suited those who were committed and wanted to improve, but it wasn't for everyone. The ones who just wanted to go through the motions, turn up late and be sloppy on the pitch were exposed. I knew immediately who they would be and it made me feel good. I didn't see why they should be allowed to take liberties, doing themselves and the club and the manager a disservice, and get away with it. Some stepped up and shaped up; some left the club.

STRUCTURE KING

Sean and I hit it off straight away. He's subsequently been quoted as saying that with me it was a case of 'opening up a door and letting him go'. Certainly, I bought into everything he did because it was exactly how I wanted to train and play football. I grew up with structure in my life, always responded well to structure and Sean was the structure king! He was the manager I had been crying out for since leaving Newcastle. I loved his meticulous sessions and he became the manager who had the biggest influence on my career.

Sean was big on trust. In one game I took responsibility as a senior pro to change the team formation, as Sean encouraged us to do when we saw a problem. Later he complimented me and I know that even if it hadn't have worked out he wouldn't have criticised or held a grudge.

He was always looking at ways to improve and give us an edge. In pre-season, Sean introduced activities that were designed to build trust and camaraderie within the group. We went to RAF camps, attended leadership and development sessions in a hotel and did orienteering, map reading, kayaking and gorge walking.

▌PEER ASSESSMENT

A couple of years in, Sean introduced what was called a peer assessment which was a powerful exercise. The whole group assembled in a large meeting room and one player was asked to go up to a separate room and write on a flipchart three words that described themselves as a player and a person, three things they thought the rest of the group would say and three things they would want the group to say.

While they were doing that the rest of us split into sub-groups of four or five to have a chat about the player – what we thought of him, what he could do better etc. Then the player came down, presented his views, got feedback from the rest of the group and there was a discussion.

When it was my turn under the spotlight I remember that two of my three terms to describe myself were 'professional' and 'technically good'. The lads agreed with that and added that they thought that in the position I played I needed to add more goals and assists to my game. They also said that I didn't spend much time in the gym and could bulk up a bit to become stronger.

I'm not sure how I would have reacted to this exercise when I was younger, but by now I was more receptive to feedback, able to reflect on what had been said, filter where necessary and make suitable changes. In fact, I didn't take action on the gym comments. I've always been slight and my body had become conditioned to playing lots of games and keeping free of injuries. I didn't want to change that. But I did take on board about upping the goals and assists; the season after I scored the most goals and was Player of the Season.

It was a pretty powerful exercise and not everybody found the feedback easy to take. I remember one player was asked what motivated him to play football and he replied 'nothing', which was quite an admission in front of his teammates and the gaffer. He didn't recover from that and soon left Doncaster.

When it came to preparing for match-days, Sean was the first one I had worked with who created a written report on the opposition; their strengths and weaknesses, individually and collectively, how they would set up tactically, their style of play. Then we'd watch videos on what we needed to do. On a Thursday we'd go through the shape of our team and how we could nullify the opposition. We'd go through throw-ins against, throw-ins for, corners against, corners for. To start with we thought the amount of detail was ridiculous. Then it became obvious that he was getting it right game after game after game, and we became converts.

That tactical attention to detail provided a strong foundation that got us results and, on top of that, we added the flair and technical quality. Not that Sean was hung up on winning. He wasn't naïve enough to think that it didn't matter, but his focus was on performances and constantly improving as individuals and as a team. Because the process was so good the performances and the wins followed – and we bought into his approach, hanging on every word.

I must also pay tribute to his number two, Richard O'Kelly, who's now assistant manager at Aston Villa. They complemented each other so well. Richard once turned up unannounced at my house when my wife and I had been unwell. He came in, had tea and a chat, made sure we were okay and had everything we needed and left. I'd never come across that before in football; someone taking time out of their day to go above and beyond. That human touch showed just how much player welfare meant to him and the club and it also showed Richard's kindness and generosity of spirit.

▮ LOST IN THE GAME

This was a prime time in my career when I had a lot of factors goings in my favour: I'd massively improved my mental performance and professionalism, I was aged between 25 and 30 (25 to 27 is generally regarded as the physical peak for a midfielder or striker), had settled down and started a family, and I was at a club with a management team and set of teammates who I trusted and enjoyed working with.

This was the most enjoyable period of my career. I went on the pitch with a massive smile on my face and no one could get near me. I couldn't wait to get to training, couldn't wait to play games.

Best of all I reached the stage where I had developed a strategy of training well through the week, preparing diligently for match-day and then trusting everything that I had been doing through the week would lead to a good performance on the pitch. The coach, Richard O'Kelly, said to me that I was at my best when I 'got lost in the game'. And he was spot on.

To get technical for a moment, what Richard was getting at was that I should trust the unconscious part of my brain. When Terry Gormley first explained the concept of conscious and unconscious thinking, the analogy that worked for me was learning to drive a car manually. When we first drive we're thinking about putting the clutch down, changing gear, steering, looking in the mirror – and our brain becomes scrambled. Then, over time, we improve and improve and improve and all of a sudden, we drive the car without thinking. Some days we end up at a destination and have no memory of how we got there.

In a similar way I had played in football matches since the age of eight and had the potential to call upon that vast amount of experience and let my muscle memory take over when the first whistle was blown on a match-day.

Of course, this was a massive reversal of my approach from my first season at Doncaster where I played in a highly conscious state, fearful and tense. I'd be looking over at the clock to see how long was left, listening to the crowd and the managers shouting at me. I was wasting time and energy on the wrong things despite a mountain of evidence that showed that it seldom led to good outcomes. Now I became more willing to let go and do things differently.

Ironically, this new-found knowledge, over time and with practice, led to me not thinking at all during the match. All the thinking and the work went on before the 90 minutes and, because I knew I had committed to training and preparation, I then just played. Learning to trust, week in, week out, what I had been doing most of my life was a game-changer

Lost in thought. I learned that it's important to think constructively but not to overthink. Ironically, on a match-day, I was at my best when I trusted my ability and just let it happen.
© HeatherKingPhotography

for me. I'd add that this approach didn't come with a 100 per cent guarantee of excellence. Even in my last season I remember a midweek game where I played out of my normal position and never got into any rhythm at all. I ended up getting subbed at half time. No one has ever nailed it for good but evenings like that became a rarity and more of the time I played in that mental state that sports performers refer to as being 'in the zone'. There are few better places to be to perform at your best. I've scored goals that I can't explain or remember because I've been absorbed in the game.

Once I started to listen and read up on the subject I found that many elite sportsmen and women operate in this way, and that gave me even more confidence. That's why I have usually thrived on the biggest occasion and why my performances became so much more consistent, averaging more than 40 games during the last 16 seasons, and starting 89 per cent of them. That didn't mean I was always an eight or a nine out of ten, but I was rarely less than a seven. Unconscious thinking and getting lost in the game helped me to achieve the standards of performance that I wanted.

'ARSENAL OF THE NORTH'

The 2006/07 season was memorable for Doncaster Rovers. On 23 December 2006, we played our final League game at Belle Vue which had been home for 84 years, and on New Year's Day 2007 we moved to the Keepmoat Stadium, celebrating with a 3-0 win over Huddersfield Town.

This all contributed to a feeling of momentum and progress and three months later we took on Bristol Rovers in the Johnstone's Paint Trophy Final in the magnificent Millennium Stadium in Cardiff. That was my first experience of a high-profile final and Grandad Coppinger, dad and a couple of friends flew

Johnstone's Paint Trophy winners in 2007 at the Millennium Stadium, and play-off winners in 2008, having beaten Leeds United at Wembley. Memorable days that whetted my appetite for the big occasion.

© Doncaster Rovers Football Club

down together to watch me. I felt an expectation to perform but relished the responsibility. The build-up, the buzz of walking out and looking around to see 59,000 spectators made me hungry for more. I thought 'wow, this is unbelievable. I love this. This is what football is all about'. We went 2-0 up, got pulled back to 2-2, went to extra time, and then won it through a header from skipper Graeme Lee in the 109th minute.

After the game I met with my friends and family to celebrate and Grandad Coppinger later said it was one of the best days of his life which, for someone who had experienced many unbelievable moments, meant a lot to me. In fact, his words have become my overriding memory of the day.

STRENGTH TO STRENGTH

The next season, 2007/08, we went from strength to strength. Quality players like Richie Wellens came to the club, we kept inching up the table and on the last game of the season if we had beaten Cheltenham we would have finished in second place and been promoted outright. In hindsight, I feel like we all thought we'd already won it and were complacent. Some of the lads had put their going-out clothes onto the coach, thinking we could go straight into Doncaster and celebrate after the game. Instead, we lost 2-1, finished in third, two points behind runners-up Nottingham Forest and fell back into the play-offs, travelling back to Doncaster with our tail between our legs.

I felt like I underperformed and used my new-found techniques to analyse my performance, work out what went wrong and consign it to the past. I decided that in future I would just play the game not the occasion – and that's what I've done ever since. In the Cheltenham game I had been too chilled; in other big games there was a danger of becoming too tense. Yet if you take away all the hype and noise it's always just a game of football, with 11 versus 11 and those two rectangles at either end of the field. It's nothing more. The players and team that handles it best tend to win the match and my learning was to trust myself and treat the 'big occasion' just like any other. Pinpointing strategies that worked for me (and understanding the ones that didn't) was a critical part of getting better.

Fortunately, I soon had the opportunity to put things right when we took on Southend United in the two-leg play-off semi-final. The first leg was unremarkable and ended goalless but I still remember the second-leg vividly: a beautiful spring evening and a packed and colourful Keepmoat Stadium. We went 2-0 up early in the game and something clicked for me. Once I scored my first goal to make it 3-0 my momentum, confidence and self-belief were huge. I was deep in a high-performance zone, able to play in a match of this magnitude as though I was still a kid playing in a park with my friends.

My second goal, with my left foot, was one of my best, and the hat-trick goal from a free-kick was the icing on the cake. I celebrated that by racing over to the bench, knowing that I had played a big part in us going to Wembley for the first time. That hat-trick was described by summariser Garry Birtles as 'three goals of the highest quality' and it was probably my most memorable and best performance as a professional footballer. An evening where everything clicked and came together. No wonder my most prized piece of sporting memorabilia is the match ball. We won that second leg 5-1 and nearly 15 years on people still come up to me and tell me where they watched the game from.

It was a defining moment in my career (how many people can say they've scored a hat-trick in the play-offs?) and gave me sky-high self-belief. That said I didn't realise the magnitude of what I'd achieved at the time. That was partly because back then the games were not as hyped and there wasn't as much media and social media scrutiny, and partly because of the manager. He made sure no one celebrated after the win and we kept our feet on the ground. Sean knew that the Southend semi-final wasn't *the* game, *the* game was the final. Winning that one was what secured the promotion. So it was 'onto the next, see you at training.' I've seen teams over-celebrate after semi-finals before and then not turn up and get beaten in the match that matters.

▌WEM-BER-LEE!

The play-off final was against our Yorkshire rivals Leeds United. I'd been to Wembley four or five times to watch Middlesbrough and they'd always lost. Then, when I watched Newcastle play Manchester United in the FA Cup Final, they also got beaten. So my track record as a spectator wasn't a great omen!

The day before our match we went to the stadium to sample the atmosphere and saw Hull City beat Bristol City 1-0 in their Championship play-off final. Afterwards, we walked around the ground and accidentally bumped into the Leeds squad. They were giggly; laughing and joking, videoing everything, and so confident (perhaps overconfident) that they were going to beat us that I sensed we had a massive opportunity.

Sure enough, we dominated the game and deserved to win by more than James Hayter's headed goal three minutes into the second half. For little Doncaster to beat the mighty Leeds was unbelievable when you think of the resources and expectations at the two clubs.

John Ryan, our chairman, came into the dressing room after we had won and the lads piled on him. I was worried about him at one point. Then the champagne and beers came out. I'm sure that achieving the massive, all-consuming ambition of promotion to the Championship was a magical moment for him and it showed how much the players cared for him.

▌SOMETHING SPECIAL

I wasn't surprised by our promotion; I always felt it was in the stars. Doncaster was buzzing as a town, the team kept improving, we'd moved to a new stadium; everything was falling into place in line with John Ryan's ambitions and we were ready to compete at Championship level. There was a feeling of being part of something special and new recruits said they felt the same.

Our first game of the 2008/09 season was at Pride Park against Derby County who had just been relegated from the Premier League, and we beat them 1-0, playing some unbelievable football. Our fans packed out the stand behind the goal, a mass of red and white, and I'll never forget that atmosphere and the sense of occasion. However, there are good reasons why the Championship is often referred to as the toughest league in the world and the Derby win was followed by a reality check: five defeats in September then four defeats and a goalless draw in October.

Despite this, morale and confidence didn't nosedive. We were learning all the time about playing at this level and even in defeat we were praised. We played at Birmingham, who had just been relegated out of the Premier League, got beaten 1-0 and their own fans applauded us off. Our resilience and togetherness helped us to keep the faith and we kept working hard in training.

By the end of December we were bottom but managed to turn things around and, starting with a 4–2 win at relegation rivals Nottingham Forest on Boxing Day, went on an undefeated run of eight games. In the end, we finished in 14th. That was no mean feat for a club with probably the tightest budget in the division.

I learned a lot about the Championship and the players who operate within it that season. Of course, as with League One and Two, the sheer number of fixtures with the Saturday-Tuesday-Saturday-Tuesday rhythm of games, and the unrelenting tempo they were played at, made it a physical endurance test. However, for me, the difference between the leagues was mainly psychological. In general, I noticed that players in the Championship were more focused, had more self-belief and were more dedicated to their profession.

▋PLAY WELL TO LEAVE

Sean O'Driscoll takes a lot of credit for the way we adjusted and stabilised within the Championship. His approach was honest and one day during that season he got four of us in his office and said, 'If you keep performing the way that you are you'll get moves from Doncaster. So forget about the results, just keep playing like this and then other teams will come and handpick you from this club.'

Some might think that's a strange approach that is counter-productive to the team. Here was a manager highlighting to his best players that there might be opportunities to secure big-money moves and leave the club! But I believe it came from a good place. What he was saying was honest and factually accurate. He was treating us with respect, putting himself in our shoes and seeing the situation from the perspective of footballers who have one career and want to achieve as much and earn as much as they can. It was also a motivational tool. He knew how football works and recognised that if we played well the team would play well – the two aspirations of progressing our careers and the team being successful were not in conflict. He knew where the club was positioned in football's hierarchy and was merely explaining the realities of the situation. Besides, he also knew that if we were sold then the money might be reinvested to refresh the squad.

Sure enough, the players he spoke to kept performing and at various times got their moves to bigger clubs. The only one who stayed was me, and more on that later.

▮FEEL-GOOD-FACTOR

The next season (2009/10) we surpassed our club-best of 14th, finishing in 12th place and amassing 60 points. That remains the highpoint for the club and we were close to getting in the play-offs. We played Blackpool, who got promoted to the Premier League, when we were only three points behind them. I think if we'd have won that game it would have taken us into the play-off positions with five or six games to go. Their manager Ian Holloway later paid homage to Sean O'Driscoll and told him that he found him an inspiration.

The Doncaster team was an absolute joy to play in. I remember opposition players asking 'how on earth has O'Driscoll got you playing like this?' We got the nickname of the 'Arsenal of the North' because we were emulating the fluid, free-flowing football of Arsene Wenger's team.

There was a feel-good factor all around the club and, in particular, in the dressing room. We enjoyed training, we enjoyed playing and the players were all on the same wavelength, driving towards the same goal. Later I spoke to Richie Wellens about that purple patch and we concluded that it was the best time of our footballing careers. From Doncaster he went to Leicester under Sven Goran Erikson and after we played them at the Keepmoat he came up to me and said, 'I don't enjoy the football at Leicester half as much as when I was here.'

I think our structure, organisation and passing were exceptional and we were building an impressive track record. For a club like Doncaster mid-table in the Championship was a great achievement, but that summer it looked like there was the ambition to go one step further. In July Billy Sharp joined, still the only time the club has paid over £1 million for a player.

At first it looked promising. Billy immediately started scoring and by November we were just outside the play-off places. However, the season became plagued by injuries to key players (we nearly had to postpone a game against Norwich City because we might not have 11 fit players) as well as poor form and we fell away in the New Year, finishing 21st and only just avoiding relegation.

That may seem like a disappointment but when you're playing for Doncaster in the Championship you are inevitably competing against clubs that have bigger budgets and bigger expectations. You have to fight for every point and survival from relegation should be seen as an achievement.

By then the O'Driscoll era had lasted five years. The team had spent three seasons in the Championship – having never reached that level before – and my performances had been consistently good. I always knew my tactical appreciation and technical ability were up to Championship standard. My body had shown it was conditioned to racking up game after game without serious injuries, and my mentality was now becoming an asset rather than a barrier. Over those five seasons I made 48, 46, 37, 42 and 42 appearances (215 in total) with 28 goals and it felt like the prime time of my career.

EYEWITNESS

SEAN O'DRISCOLL

Sean played over 600 games in midfield for Fulham and Bournemouth, before moving into coaching and management. As you've just read, I immediately bought into what Sean brought to Doncaster and he became a massively positive influence on me during his five years with the club, a time when I played some of my best football.

In addition to Doncaster, he has managed Bournemouth, Nottingham Forest, Bristol City and Walsall. At the time of writing he is head of coaching and learning at Portsmouth's academy.

JAMES'S CHARACTER – 'I'd describe James as committed, creative and enigmatic. Myself and the coaching staff knew him as a player from his Exeter days and always wondered what his back story was. He wasn't difficult to get to know but he intrigued us; an interesting character who thought differently about football. He wanted to understand stuff rather than just take everything at face value. You know going into clubs some people will fly with it, some just want to be told what to do and some people will struggle with it. I don't think we were aware at the time that we were having that much of a positive influence on him, although his performances would suggest that.

'We thought he was a cultured footballer with enormous potential, and we trusted him to do more than he thought he could do. We weren't content to let him play on the wing and just stand there and do one or two good things a game. We got him more involved. We also tried to bring in like-minded players, who were on the same wavelength, and that helped him enormously.'

PROBLEM SOLVING – 'We decided the principles we wanted to play to and tried to make the structure of the team as robust as we could. But we also gave the players flexibility. In training sessions we set players problems on the pitch, letting them work out how to solve it. We had some really bright lads who would lead the others. Sometimes their solutions weren't quite what I wanted but I liked it when they took the ownership and responsibility to actually do something within the constraints of the practice.

'We did that an awful lot because when they played on a Saturday we could scream and shout all we wanted but nine times out of ten they couldn't hear us. We gave the players autonomy to alter the system on the pitch to counteract the problems we had without taking away from the way we wanted to play. That was the type of thing that James was really good at. I remember a couple of times he shouted over to the touchline and asked, "Can we change to 4-4-2?" or something like that. My response was, "If you think that's right then do it." That was a learning process for the players because sometimes they'd change too soon or because it was the easiest thing to do. Sometimes we might not let it happen, but if we did, as long as they had a reason for the decision, even if we lost the game, we wouldn't come down on them. That would be ridiculous. That's where the trust comes into it. If we asked them to do something then we didn't judge them on whether we won, lost or drew. We judged them on whether it was the right thing to do.'

PERFORMANCES ABOVE RESULTS – 'We didn't really go after results, we went after performances. I think that landed with James. As a player you can get judged on whether you win or lose, and it's sometimes a bit galling when you've played really well and you've lost and people only want to talk about the negatives. One of my quotes was, "If somebody can tell me how to win playing badly then we'll be doing it week in, week out to help keep our jobs."'

LEADERSHIP GROUP (a small group of experienced players who met after every game on a Monday and filtered down messages to everybody else) – 'We started a leadership group but James wasn't comfortable in it. He argued – and in hindsight I think he was quite right – that we had created an elite group, another layer, that almost set them aside from the team. He didn't think that was the right thing to do. We accepted but didn't agree with his reasons when he stepped out of it, but now I can see his point more clearly.'

PEER ASSESSMENT EXERCISE (an exercise when players and management provide feedback on each other) – 'It's easier when you're in charge and you've got your feet under the table, and when the group trusts each other and is comfortable with it. The fact that I went first in the exercise and was the guinea pig helped. It was good that the players felt confident enough to tell me their views on me as a manager.

'The assessments usually ended up with some positives. It was like a support mechanism; for instance, if a player wanted to get stronger and work in the gym but lacked the motivation to do it, somebody would team up with him and say, "Okay, every time I go in the gym I'm going to grab you, and we'll go together." That type of thing was really beneficial.'

COMMUNITY – 'When we first joined Doncaster they had been successful and were mid-table League One, so the next step was to take all the good stuff and move it on. People trusted one another; not just the team, it was the whole club. We tried to bring everybody together and connect with the local community. We went into Doncaster Prison and things like that because we thought it was important. As a group we were trying to influence a conurbation and do things that helped people be proud of their football club and that came through in the way we played. It went hand in hand. We were committed and wouldn't cancel a community project on a Tuesday if we lost on a Saturday. If I had to pick one reason why we were successful at Doncaster it would be that.'

MINDSET – 'I think what goes on between the ears is the most important thing. Without a professional mindset nothing else works. When we talk about great players in any sport then you'll always talk about intangibles such as resilience or commitment or confidence – all the things that make up a human being. The fact that James played so long was testament to his mental strength and if he can share the way he thinks about football and what drove him on to other players it would undoubtedly help them reach their potential.

'The importance of mentality also applies to managers and coaches. Many could write books on the technical and tactical but the most successful ones are the most robust, can take the knocks, can treat everybody the same and have a good work-life balance.'

ANALYSIS

TEAMWORK AND CONSISTENCY

If a student was writing a university dissertation on the traits of high-performing teams then the first four and a half seasons of Doncaster Rovers under the management of Sean O'Driscoll would make a perfect case study.

We played against clubs with playing squads of established reputations and proven tactical, technical and physical qualities – and somehow we kept beating them. During that period we consistently punched above our weight, and that was down to the magic created by astute management and a bunch of good pros, with a good mentality and togetherness.

That's so important, particularly as you go down the leagues, because what brings success, in my opinion, is effort, commitment and team spirit. The players are still accomplished in their individual roles but they're not as good technically or physically as the Premier League superstars. They don't have the breath-taking quality of a Kevin De Bruyn or Mohammed Salah to win matches on their own. So success tends to come from the excellence of the group rather than individual brilliance.

I can't emphasise enough that young, aspiring footballers will benefit from realising that football is not like golf, tennis and other largely individual sports; personal performance is only of value if it helps the team.

▌DRIVING FORCE

In defining the ingredients that created the successful period at Doncaster we need to start with the leadership and management of the chairman, John Ryan, the manager, Sean O'Driscoll, and his assistant, Richard O'Kelly. They set the tone and led from the front.

John put all his time and commitment to our success. He had a clear and ambitious vision and was able to communicate it in a way that inspired others. He was fully behind the management team and the playing squad and everyone in the club shared a common purpose. As I covered in the section on visualisation, having clarity for the desired result is an essential starting point, whether it's one person or a whole organisation.

If you look at the likes of Leicester City when they won the Premier League – in fact, all the big clubs that have done well – there's always a driving force behind them. John Ryan provided that at Doncaster Rovers, and you could feel it as a player.

John's energy and fervour was only matched by Richard O'Kelly, who, closer to the players, was also incredibly upbeat. He knew how to pick you up and was so bloody positive that it almost got on your nerves! But we knew it was all meant in the best possible way. If you worked for Doncaster Rovers in any capacity during this period you would have enjoyed it. There was a sense of fun alongside all the hard work.

More understated but incredibly influential was Sean O'Driscoll. I've found that the best managers are like him: consistent in their expectations, their actions and their communication.

Sean felt that if we concentrated on following our ways of working and continually improved as individuals and as a team then eight or nine times out of ten we would perform well and get the right result. Again, I loved that, and I believe there is a broader lesson about management in the workplace: don't get too distracted by or over-react to the headline numbers; concentrate on trusting the process and doing the right things. Whereas some other managers I've played for only cared about the result. If we lost then we got a verbal hammering and it was as though we had become the worst team ever. If we won then it was smiles all round and we were ready to take on the world!

John, Sean, Richard: the whole management team at Doncaster, in their different ways, combined to provide an environment that was conducive to success.

▮FOCUS

The links between the boardroom, the coaching and management staff and the players were strong, with a spirit that is very rare to find in professional sport –

and we should add that there was an unusually strong chemistry with the club's loyal supporters and the broader community around Doncaster. Sean mentioned in his Eyewitness account that they were critical to our success. Certainly, it all felt together, joined up and focused in the same direction and I want to highlight characteristics that were essential to creating that bond throughout the club:

RESPECT

Firstly, there was mutual and genuine respect between the directors, management, players, supporters and community. We understood how we were all inter-dependent and how each played a critical part in the club's fortunes. I've seen managers who lost the dressing room and were treated with disdain, directors who interfered and didn't support their manager, players who were cynical about their fans and the community they represented. Don't get me wrong, it doesn't mean that if you work with someone you have to be their best mate. Respect is different from friendship; and more important in my opinion.

TRUST

It was equally important that trust existed in the boardroom, the dugout, the dressing room and on the pitch, and that no one's hidden agendas and personal aspirations were in conflict with what the club was trying to achieve.

In particular, I valued that I could trust my teammates. The ideal is that you look around the dressing room and see players who you know will dig in when the going gets tough, will run back for you, run forward, and are going to look after the ball if you give it to them and make the right decisions. You want to know that they're going to give everything for you and the team. However, I've played in teams when trust is lacking and performances suffer – and once the trust is gone it's incredibly difficult to rebuild.

The exercises that Sean put us through in pre-season were designed to build that trust and the players he brought had characters who maintained those relationships; they were all on the same wavelength.

▌HONESTY

Finally, honesty, which is reliant on trust and respect. Everyone needs to feel able to voice their opinions and be open and honest with each other. The peer assessment exercise was an example of how this could help the team. Disagreements and conflict may occur in any group but if trust and respect also exist they will be amicably resolved without damaging the relationships. Sean led from the front on this. He was honest with the players and if one of them voiced a critical opinion he listened and held no grudges. Everyone knew where they stood.

▌TEAM-FOCUSED

Because of the trust, respect and honesty the players tended to recognise other people's contributions, unselfishly supporting and covering for each other and putting the team first.

There are so many facets to that, on and off the pitch:

- Sometimes accepting that you've not been selected in the starting 11 but supporting the team rather than moaning or sulking.
- Playing out of position to help win a football match.
- Working hard without the ball.
- Playing the unselfish pass when in a good position rather than a speculative shot.
- 'Taking one for the team' and committing a professional foul and getting a yellow card to stop a dangerous opposition counter-attack.

The players who excel in these traits can be more admired in the dressing room than by supporters because their work often goes unnoticed. Over that high-performing period the Doncaster squad shone in this area and new signings, such as Brian Stock, James Hayter and James O'Connor, fitted in with the ethos, never threatening to jeopardise the dynamics of the group. If you played for us you knew your job and you did it unselfishly. We had no individualists.

A decade or more later that's become the norm. Even the superstars, no matter how skilled, can't just do their own thing. Everyone has to play for the team. Harry Kane is a perfect example; the work he does off the ball is unbelievable. Liverpool's front three of Mohammed Salah, Roberto Firmino and Sadio Mane are the same. Managers are expecting more, and it's become widely recognised that flair players can also work hard.

Of course, each player at Doncaster under Sean O'Driscoll had their unique qualities and attributes but I believe respect and trust, honesty and team-focus were the cornerstones of our success. Because we had them in abundance we were able to deal with setbacks and turn in consistently good performances that helped push us on to achieve the highest league position in the club's history, despite having a minimal budget compared to other teams in the Championship.

▮CONSISTENCY

The key word in that last paragraph is 'consistently'. Because of those cornerstones our physical and mental routines, motivation, performances and recovery were consistent. It's inevitable in professional sport that you get high and lows, wins and losses, but as a group we never got too up or too down. There weren't bust-ups, dramas and rollercoaster emotional highs and lows. We just got on with it. The manager knew what he would get from us and I, for example, felt confident that we could all be relied upon to do our bit every match-day. In short, we had a pro mindset.

With that in mind, my advice to the aspiring footballer is to recognise the part you play in creating the magic and success that comes with team spirit. You don't play in isolation. It's not all about you. Play for the team as well as yourself.

TAKEAWAYS

- Appreciate that football is a team sport. It's not all about you. Your personal performance is only of value if it helps the team.

- Respect, trust and honesty are the foundations of high performing teams. Play your part in creating that culture.

- Recognise other people's contributions, unselfishly support and cover for each other and always try and put the team first.

LEADERSHIP AND COMMUNICATION

7

CHANGE AND EXPERIMENTS

IN JUNE 2011, along with Mark Wilson, James O'Connor, other Rovers staff and local Doncaster businessmen David Plant and Brian Butcher, I walked the 62-mile Inca Trek to Machu Picchu, raising almost £50,000 for charity. It was an eye-opening experience and allowed me to reflect on where I was and where I wanted to be.

There was a feeling of change in the air. I was aware that Dave Penney had rejected some bids for me when he was the manager and thought that the board and Sean O'Driscoll may have done the same. I'd been playing well for several years so, to be honest, I would have been surprised if no one had come in for me. By now, the others whom Sean had spoken to had all got their moves and, at the age of 30 years old, I needed to work out if I saw my long-term future at Doncaster.

Then Ipswich Town put in a bid. My understanding is that initially the fee suggested by our chairman John Ryan was £500,000, which Ipswich were willing to pay. Doncaster bumped it up to £750,000, Ipswich agreed again, and Doncaster bumped it once more, to £1m, a price where it looked like they would allow the move to happen.

In truth, I found Ipswich an attractive option. They had been in the Premier League and were renowned for playing good football. I went to their training ground, had a tour around Portman Road and had a chat with Charlie Woods, a coach who I knew from our Newcastle days, their manager, Paul Jewell, and their chairman. We discussed a contract (which would have improved my wages by three or four times) and then the ball was in Doncaster's court.

I met John Ryan at Wetherby Services, amongst all the smells from take-away and fast-food restaurants, to discuss my future. Ipswich had asked me to put in a transfer request and kick up a fuss to try and get the move going but it was clear that despite the increasing valuations John Ryan was reluctant to let me leave – and, in truth, I wasn't desperate to go either. He offered a new, three-year contract and a testimonial (a non-competitive match to honour a player for his ten-year service) at the end of it. I valued how I'd been treated at Doncaster and the chairman made a persuasive offer, so I decided to stay and on 21 July 2011 signed a three-year contract with a testimonial at the end.

I know a lot of players have come and gone in the time that I've been at Doncaster, sometimes for more money to one of the so-called 'bigger' clubs. Then three or four months down the line they're not playing, not enjoying the football and they wish they'd have stayed. I never wanted to go to a club and be a bit-part player. Yes, I subsequently went to Nottingham Forest for four months on loan but that was due to the finances of the club. I always knew I would come back.

Over the years the club matched my ambition so I never felt a reason to go. I could have gone for more money but I've never played football because of the financial gain. My motivation was to enjoy my football, be part of something meaningful where I could leave a legacy and make sure my family was happy. I know that sounds corny and when I say it people must think I'm stupid, but everybody's different and that's why I stayed when others had left.

That said, my view might have been different if a Premier League team had come in for me. In an ideal world a move back to Newcastle would have been a dream come true now that I was in a much better place psychologically. However, when you get released from a Premier League club it's so difficult to then work your way back up to that level.

▌THE EXPERIMENT

After a challenging end to the 2010/11 campaign – when we nosedived to 21st place after a run of injuries and poor form – the next season started in a similar style. On the first day we were one-up away at Brighton with seven minutes to go before injuries, with all the substitutions already made, reduced us to ten men. Two late goals turned a likely win into a defeat. Ten days later we outplayed Nottingham Forest. At half time Jonathan Greening, who was playing for them said, 'You're unbelievable. I'd love to play in your team. You're like Barcelona.' Yet we somehow lost one-nil.

We were playing well but not getting results and the weeks went on without a win. This was also a season when the club's approach to recruitment began to change and a few colourful characters joined who didn't buy into Sean and his philosophy – and at the end of September 2011, having taken one point from the first seven games of the season, the manager was sacked.

CHANGE OF DIRECTION

Despite the run of results, Sean's departure came as a massive shock. I always said as soon as we lost him we would struggle unless he was replaced by somebody with a similar management style. Remember that there aren't many Sean O'Driscolls around; they were always going to be big, big boots to fill.

The choice for his replacement was Dean Saunders, previously manager of Wrexham from the Conference Premier. Saunders was a well-known figure within football thanks to a playing career spanning more than 600 games for 12 different clubs, including Derby County, Liverpool and Aston Villa, as well as 75 games and 22 goals for Wales. Those stats demanded respect. I'd liked him as a player and I tried to take it at face value and find the positives. But, in truth, I found it difficult. I wanted continuity of the approach that had worked for five years, yet it was immediately apparent that O'Driscoll and Saunders were chalk and cheese. You would have struggled to find two managers who were more different.

I would accept that it was difficult for Dean because he was an inexperienced manager at this level, replacing a highly competent and proven professional. His philosophy was old school, bringing in new signings and saying, 'We've got better players than them so we'll win.'

The fact that he was a personable guy who had been an elite footballer wasn't enough for me. Just because you've been an elite player doesn't mean you will become an elite manager. Although it's the same industry it's an entirely different skillset. To be at my best I needed structure and discipline, to know that I was trusted and that the gaffer considered me an integral part of the starting 11, as I believe my performances over the previous five seasons had merited. But I didn't get that from Dean. I always felt he managed off the cuff and that I wasn't his kind of player. That said, to be honest, probably his biggest sin, in my eyes, was that he wasn't Sean O'Driscoll.

I remember our first away game with Dean as manager against Peterborough. We were losing one-nil at half time and the lads had plenty to say as we came in. Dean was like, 'Whoa, whoa, whoa. There's too many chiefs in here. I'm the manager so I'm the one who speaks.' Before we'd been encouraged to take responsibility, speak up and find our own solutions.

On Fridays at training we'd have five-a-sides and Dean decided that the player who played the best or scored the best goal would get a prize. One day he brought a thoroughbred racehorse to the training ground, ridden by director of football Mickey Walker. He announced that the winner of that day's prize would get shares in the racehorse! Ultimately he awarded it to Brian Carey, his assistant manager, who had played in the five-a-side, which felt like a bit of a fix!

In those Friday sessions Dean joined in and, then, on the journey to away games, he would get on the microphone at the front of the team bus and hold court, starting by giving out the ratings for the five-a-side as if he was the local reporter. He'd go through both teams: 'Brian Stock, six out of ten, bang average. James Coppinger, seven out of 10, just about okay.' Then he'd always say, 'Dean Saunders: nine out of 10, man of the match, ran the game.' He'd have people in stitches and was undoubtedly funny; an extrovert, a joker, a character. I don't know whether he always meant it, but it was quite comical.

Yet, at the same time, he had inherited a group who were there for football, not comedy. So when he was taking training sessions and trying drills that didn't come off we looked at each other with quizzical expressions.

▋BLUE-CHIP RECRUITS

The change of direction wasn't only reflected in the personalities and approaches of the managers. The previous transfer policy was also ripped up and replaced.

When Saunders joined, the summer transfer window had just closed and the club looked to bring in new, high-profile players with proven track records on short-term deals using loans and free transfers. At the end of September 32-year-old full-back Pascal Chimbonda joined on a free transfer. He had Premier League experience, having once been signed for around £4 million by Tottenham Hotspur and for £2 million by Blackburn Rovers. A week later 29-year-old Herita Ilunga joined on loan from West Ham. That month also saw 30-year-old El Hadji Diouf joining on a free. He was another with experience at the top level with Liverpool, Bolton, Sunderland and Blackburn. And in November 34-year-old Habib Beye joined on loan from Aston Villa.

This complete change of direction with management and recruitment became known as 'The Experiment'. In total ten players were brought in, often at reduced wages, keen to put themselves in the shop window in the hope that their displays would seal a permanent deal elsewhere.

There was no doubting their blue-chip quality but they had passed their peak and had less emotional connection to the club or the other players. Their hunger and drive had waned as they pursued other interests outside of football. As a result, not all of them set the highest professional standards.

For instance, Habib Beye lived in France and flew in for matches. He'd arrive with his suitcase, train on

Thursday and Friday and play on Saturday. If we had a Tuesday game he'd turn up on the day of the match. How can you justify that?

He was a centre-back and the others who played in that position trained all week, giving it 100 per cent, trying to get into the team and secure the next contract because they wanted to do well for themselves and their families. Yet Habib could play poorly on a Saturday and still always get selected in front of them. That wasn't his fault – he didn't select the team – but it was clear that he was being picked on reputation rather than performances.

▮TOXIC DRESSING ROOM

It probably wouldn't be a surprise to learn that the dynamic in the dressing room changed. The O'Driscoll group had been programmed to a certain way of playing and working. We were all about the team and togetherness, on and off the pitch, and the results suggested it had worked for us. Then, all of a sudden, that playbook got ripped up. Within two, three, four weeks the cracks were appearing and what had been built up so carefully was being dismantled.

I can't really speak for the incomers but my general observations would be that they came in, did their own thing, didn't work hard, didn't feel what we felt for the club and weren't motivated by team success.

In my opinion, if you're employed by Doncaster Rovers Football Club you have to come in every day and give your best. Every team I've played in that's been successful had everybody pulling in the same direction. Without that it's almost impossible and, in this group, one half of us wanted to work together and the other half didn't. It felt like we had two cliques.

This tested my professionalism. I tried not to be affected by these external factors, to just concentrate on what I could control, turn up and play my football. I tried to conduct myself in the right way and not get drawn into sniping and apportioning blame. I went about my business quietly and I very rarely spoke to Dean about it because I didn't believe I could influence what was happening and would have just put myself to the sword if I had been too outspoken. However, I imagine that my body language communicated how I felt. It was arguably the hardest and most difficult time I had at Doncaster.

▌NO HAPPY ENDINGS

When you play at Championship level you need more than individual quality.

I never looked around the dressing room on a match-day and thought 'yeah, today we're going to win'. Every time we played it was a toss of a coin whether we were going to perform or not. Yes, we had quality players – and sometimes El Hadji Diouf would score a worldie and win us a game – but when we played teams that were organised and had the togetherness that we lacked then we struggled. It was incredibly frustrating and the majority of the players were like me, coming in every day in disbelief about what was going on. It was only going to end one way. Sure enough, we finished bottom, relegated out of the Championship. It was labelled as an experimental season and the evidence was clear: the experiment failed.

WATER BOTTLES, HORSES AND TOYS R US

Having been relegated at the end of the 2011/12 season, Doncaster needed to offload players to reduce the wage bill and release funds to bring other players in. I became a subject of interest from Ipswich (again) and Barnsley but it was the option to go on loan to Nottingham Forest that most attracted my interest.

I used to support Forest as a kid, Sean O'Driscoll had just become their manager and they played in the Championship. Besides, I wouldn't have to move location and, as I was now 31 years old, I knew Forest wouldn't offer me anything permanently and I'd come back at the end of the loan. It just felt right, an opportunity to get out of an environment that I wasn't enjoying.

I remember I was on the team bus on the way to a match at Yeovil on the August 2012 Deadline Day when word came in of Forest's offer. I spoke to my agent on the phone and it was agreed that I would be dropped off at a service station and he would come and pick me up. I think by then Dean Saunders wanted me to be as far away from him as possible. As I got off he got the microphone, winked at me, and said, 'Thank **** he's gone.' He said it as a joke; deep down I suspect he meant it.

We went to the City Ground and I signed, joining up with ex-Rovers players Simon Gillett and Billy

Sharp as well as my former manager. It was a real eye-opener for me to go to a club of that stature, yet I could also understand why they weren't as successful as they had been in the past because there were some elements – though not so extreme – of the problems we had suffered at Rovers: some not pulling in the same direction, some not working as hard as they could.

Certainly, I think Sean found it difficult to re-create the magic of Doncaster. This group were less inclined to buy into his meticulous and idiosyncratic approach, perhaps because they were already conditioned to other ways, were streetwise within the professional set-up and more difficult to impress.

▌ WATER BOTTLES

The players at Forest were treated like kings in comparison to Doncaster and I remember Sean telling me that they had a guy specifically allocated to take out the water bottles onto the training pitch. He couldn't believe it and changed it so that everybody had to look after their own. The players just couldn't believe that decision, simply couldn't get their heads around it. Getting them to take their own water bottle out proved to be challenging so I'm not sure they *got* Sean in the way that his group of disciples at Doncaster did.

And I'm not sure management and the board were as one either. After just five months in charge of the club, hours after a 4–2 victory over Leeds United, Sean was sacked and not long after I also left and returned to Doncaster.

ALL BETS ARE OFF

I was at Forest when I became involved in an incident that placed an unfair and regrettable stain on my character. I wasn't a big gambler, but a friend of mine who I played with tipped me off that a horse was an absolute certainty to finish outside the top three in a race. I couldn't understand that – I'd never gambled that way before – and he talked me through how to put that kind of strange bet on. I remember speaking to my wife at the time, discussing whether I should do it.

In the end, I placed the bet and the horse won! I couldn't believe it and thought I was being wound up. I gave my friend a bit of stick and that was that; at least until three years later when I got a call from the British Horseracing Association. It emerged that a couple had spoken to the jockey before the race and were being investigated for fixing horse races.

One day after training at Forest I showered, changed, got my food and drink for lunch, sat down and saw on the Sky Sports ticker-tape at the bottom of the television screen the breaking news that I was one of a group who had been found guilty of corrupt and fraudulent practices in gambling on horses to lose on betting exchanges.

It was a real cold sweat moment and soul-destroying for me, my family and everyone associated with me. Over the years I'd created a reputation as a good and honest pro, yet overnight people were judging me and assuming that I was part of a group who were fixing horseraces. That was wrong. I'd been innocently roped in on this one occasion, placing just one bet, and losing my money.

I was advised not to say anything by my lawyers so I couldn't defend myself and tell my story. But they are the facts. Despite this, the British Horseracing Association banned me from horse-racing activities for three years, which was no hardship. It brought to an end an unfair and stressful incident that still leaves a sour taste. It was another test of my resilience and it was fortunate that by now I was mature, self-aware and knowledgeable enough about my thinking habits to not worry and fret so much that it significantly affected my mental health and well-being.

No surprise, though, that I was happy to draw a line under my time at Nottingham Forest and get back to Doncaster.

❙GOOD PROS AND A WARRIOR

In the meantime Rovers had addressed the issues caused by 'The Experiment' and changed course again, reverting to a more tried-and-tested approach that had proven to be successful before in the lower leagues. Out went the blue-chip star names, in came a bunch of ambitious, good pros such as Rob Jones, who'd just been promoted with Sheffield Wednesday, Jamie McCombe, David Cotterill and Iain Hume.

Dean Saunders had begun to mould a group that bought into his ways and wanted to play for him and the club. By the time I returned, midway through the season, the team was sitting at the top of League

One, although Dean went to take over as manager at Wolverhampton Wanderers.

No matter, I could see that there was a working atmosphere, everybody had a common goal to get promoted and everybody believed that was possible.

It helped that we had an absolute warrior to lead us. That season Rob Jones gave the best captain/player performance I've ever seen – and at some points he was almost the manager, along with Brian Flynn, after Dean Saunders left. He scored goals; cleared balls left, right and centre; dragged everybody along with him and was a leader of men. It wasn't just on the pitch either. Everyone looked up to him, everybody listened when he spoke – and because he was playing so well he could back his words up. Everything he touched that season turned to gold. He's the best captain, the best leader, I've played under.

He drove the club forward and stood out, but senior pros like Neil Sullivan and Dean Furman who had been there, seen it, and done it supported him. We didn't play the best football, we weren't the most attractive to watch but we knew how to win football games.

I've always gravitated to that culture and enjoyed the responsibility of knitting play together on the pitch and getting the team to gel. After my return in January, I played every game and, in doing so, reached the personal landmark of 300 League appearances for Doncaster, one of only ten in the club's history.

It had never entered my head that we would immediately bounce back from relegation, yet we only had to draw against Brentford on the last day of the season to get promoted.

GOOSEBUMPS

After 94 minutes – in the last seconds of added time – the game was still goalless and it looked like an immediate return to the Championship was imminent, but that was before one of the most incredible finales to a promotion showdown the League has ever seen!

Brentford were awarded a penalty! If they missed we were promoted; if they scored they went up and we'd drop down into the playoffs. So I stood on the edge of the box, hands-on-hips, thinking 'I might have to travel all the way from Guisborough to Doncaster for training for another three weeks!'

That's not all. It was also in my mind that I'd just bought a pair of football goals for the kids, and when I walked out of the shop I realised the woman hadn't charged us for one of them. I was intending to go back and tell her but hadn't had the chance. So when that penalty was given, I thought this was some kind of karma; that it happened because I had underpaid Toys R Us! In amongst the bedlam I stood on the edge of the box feeling guilty!

Then things got even more surreal, like an out of body experience. Brentford's Marcello Trotta slammed the penalty against the crossbar and their players collapsed on the floor in frustration and despair! The ball bounced down and got cleared to Billy Paynter, on the right, on the halfway line. Now the break was on and I spotted the opportunity. One Brentford lad was running back, but I started running past him, up to the other end of the pitch with Billy.

Billy was a typical goal-hungry striker; and I never expected him to pass to me. But this time he spotted me, squared it – I took a touch because I was surprised – and I tapped it in. Goosebumps! I threw my shirt into the crowd and then had to put somebody else's shirt on to get on the pitch again. And the full-time whistle went! We went up as champions, one point above Bournemouth! It's probably the best feeling I've ever had in football; a once-in-a-lifetime moment that will stick with me

Carnage! Bedlam! A missed last-minute penalty at one end, a breakaway and a goal at the other. Goosebumps! Promotion!
© Doncaster Rovers Football Club

forever. That's why all the sacrifices, all the hard work, all the dedication is worth it. That's why the drama of sport is so addictive and gripping. There are no scripts.

SNAKES AND LADDERS

Doncaster fans could never complain that life was boring and this period of the club's history was full of twists and turns, ups and downs, albeit most weren't as dramatic as the last-minute drama at Brentford, which had reversed relegation in the previous season.

Optimism that we would be able to enter a period of stability in the Championship proved to be unfounded. The next four seasons we played snakes and ladders: relegated down into League One in 2013/14, relegated further, into League Two in 2015/16 and then promoted back into League One in 2016/17. So for five out of six seasons we were either promoted or relegated!

In some ways the excitement of a potential promotion or the threat of relegation is what you want as a player. At least you have something to play for in every match instead of that 'on the beach' feeling when the games are comparatively meaningless. However, those ups and downs play with your head and bouncing back from relegation is one of the toughest tasks in football. During those rollercoaster six seasons I played 236 games (despite spending several months on loan at Nottingham Forest) so no one at the club was in a better position to know how to deal with the instability from a psychological perspective.

The approach that I took was a variation of the 24-hour re-set button that I used to put games behind me. I allowed a short period where I basked in the joy of promotion or wallowed in the despair of relegation – then I put the past behind me, re-set my goals and focused on the new challenge of competing in a different division.

▌DISTRACTED

However, relegation in 2013/14 was particularly hard to take. Under the new management of Paul Dickov we beat Leeds 2-1 at Elland Road at the end of March with seven games to go to move nine points from safety and we thought we were home and dry. Instead of making sure that we stayed focused and concentrated on our own business, we became distracted, looking over our shoulder, seeing how other teams were getting on, hoping that the results went our way.

April was disastrous: defeats against Birmingham, Bolton, Ipswich, Derby and Reading and a goalless draw at Millwall. So we went into the last game of the season needing a draw at Leicester City, who had just got promoted to the Premier League. We were doing well up until the 75th minute when David Nugent scored a penalty. If Birmingham lost we would have still been okay, but having been 2-0 down with 12 minutes to go they equalised in the 90th minute and we got relegated.

Fine margins yet it wasn't anybody else's fault but ours. We should have done more that season and something I learned from that was not to worry and focus on other teams. That mindset of 'controlling the controllables' didn't just apply at a personal level, it applied to teams as well.

It was little consolation that I had become only the fifth Rovers player to reach 350 League appearances when I played against Nottingham Forest in March 2014.

■ ONE DIRECTION, NEW DIRECTION

The next season – 2014/15 – was rare because we had nothing to play for at the end, finishing in a mid-table 13th place. The highpoint was my testimonial at the Keepmoat with One Direction's Louis Tomlinson taking a leading role. As a Doncaster lad he had a big

My testimonial with chairman John Ryan and One Direction's Louis Tomlinson.

© Doncaster Rovers Football Club

affiliation with the club and played in the reserves. So Team Tomlinson played Team Coppinger in a friendly match. I went round to every corporate box with him before the game and there was no doubt from the reaction of the supporters who the star was! I was merely the support act! It was an insight for me into fame and I can't speak highly enough of how this down to earth, humble guy dealt with the attention.

By the start of the 2015/16 season it was clear that the club was in a rut and needed a new direction. Following a poor start manager Paul Dickov was sacked, replaced a month later by Darren Ferguson. There was also a change in the boardroom as John Ryan stood down.

That said, for a while things got worse before they got better. I did have the honour, in November 2015, of making my 469th senior appearance for Rovers, which meant I replaced Colin Douglas as the player who had made the most senior appearances for the club. That was no consolation, though, when a terrible run of 13 defeats and four draws from 17 games (having been on the edge of the playoff positions at the New Year) at the start of 2016 saw us relegated back to League Two. That was painful for everyone at the club but perhaps it had to happen to allow the opportunity to reboot and restructure.

LEADING FROM THE BACK

Darren Ferguson was adamant that he would get the club back to League One and in the summer of 2016 the club made some great signings, in particular the centre-forward, John Marquis. He was just what we needed: although, at 24 years old, he wasn't a senior pro he took responsibility and grew frustrated at times because he demanded so much from himself and others. It got heated at times but I much preferred that to somebody who didn't care and went through the motions. That season John was top goalscorer, got Player of the Season and we got promoted back into League One with five games to go.

This promotion felt special to me.

Part of that was because I was able to honour my grandad (Coppinger) who had lost his battle to cancer just before the season started. I remember that the team he supported, Middlesbrough, had just been promoted back to the Premier League and I bought him their new shirt and took it to him in hospital. In contrast, three or four days before he passed away, I promised him that Doncaster would get promoted straight back up into League One. That gave me an all-consuming drive to do well.

This was a sign of how much my mindset had developed over the years. Rather than becoming consumed by grief and feeling sorry for myself, as I had in the past, I viewed his passing as a source of motivation. Every day that season I drew inspiration from his life.

▌500 CLUB

By now I was heavily into goal setting as a way of giving me purpose, and all the ones I set that season were achieved. The team did indeed get promoted back to League One, I was named in the PFA League Two Team of the Season at the age of 36. I got nominated for Rovers' Player of the Season, scored ten goals and contributed 15 assists.

I also passed the 500-game mark for Rovers in September 2016, celebrating the milestone by scoring in a 5–1 away victory over Morecambe. A lot of travelling fans made the trip that day and I felt like I had to perform. I visualised scoring and it felt like it had to be. I also scored in my 501st game when the celebrations

Cloud Nine. A goal to celebrate
my 500th game for Doncaster at
Morecambe.

© AHPiXPhotography

Vantage
bookies.c
BET
estate agents
Jessops
£999
THE INSURANCE CENTRE
Personal Commercial
01524 848506
BLAIR
17
MARQUIS
9
© AHPiXPhotography

continued in a home game at the Keepmoat. It was arguably one of my best seasons.

By now, as my footballing career entered its final years, portraits of me were dotted around the Rovers' training ground, that last-minute goal against Brentford was pictured on a mural as you walk up to the Legends Lounge in the Keepmoat Stadium, and a banner of me overlooked the pitch in the South Stand. In truth this attention made me feel uncomfortable. I have never enjoyed having my name in lights and would prefer people to simply view me as a humble, good professional who always gave his all for the club. Yet over the years I had built a status and positive reputation at the club which I was proud of. But football is a hard-nosed business with minimal sentiment and when Darren Ferguson took over he got me and Richie Wellens (who had returned to the club from Leicester City a few seasons earlier) in his office and said, 'Look, you're both getting on, I can't play you both in the same team for obvious reasons.' He was more or less saying I'm going to have to get rid of one of you, and although I had (and still have) total admiration and respect for Richie my immediate response was to think 'Bring it on', I want this challenge.

Darren had been unsure on his arrival of how much of a contribution I would be able to make and I wanted to prove to him that I was good enough. Richie actually left the club in January 2016 as I stayed and moved to the forefront of Darren's plans.

CAPTAIN COPPINGER

The other reason that promotion stood out for me was that Darren ended up making me captain. I think he saw me as dedicated and that was the main reason he chose me. He wanted me to set the standard, particularly during training. People don't see the Monday to Friday sessions but they set the tone and create a platform to perform on match-days. His decision was a massive incentive for me to keep pushing myself and others.

I had worked with some really good captains and studied how they did it, but I tried to put my stamp on the role and play to my strengths rather than copying anyone else. The key element of my approach was to lead by example, both on and off the pitch. I liked and tried to follow the quote by John Wooden which states that 'The most powerful leadership tool you have is your own personal example'. I was acutely aware of that and I made sure that for the good of the team I did things right and went above and beyond. Of course, I also did this for myself – to perform well and prolong my career as much as possible – but I hoped that my approach would be infectious and others would follow.

I tried to work the hardest and be the most enthusiastic in training, whether it was a five-a-side on a Friday, a sprinting drill or running out to a cone. If the others were watching this old guy putting in the hard yards then they knew they couldn't get away with going through the motions! Certainly, I

was acutely aware that I would have no credibility or authority in the role if I turned up late, was lifeless or behaved negatively at training. It would have given them a reason to take their eye off the ball.

Why waste time being average? Giving it 100 per cent and putting in the hard yards at training.
© HeatherKingPhotography

More broadly I tried to be:

- open to new ideas
- keen to offer encouragement to others when we were struggling and showing the stomach for a fight
- committed, energetic and hard-working on the pitch, playing my best when the team most needed it

- respectful of teammates, the sport and supporters
- diligent in my off-field commitments, aware that I was representing the whole club within the community

In general, I was an understated captain who gave other players such as Tommy Rowe, Andy Butler and Matty Blair the responsibility to take the lead. They were all senior players who helped me. It made my job a lot easier.

Occasionally, though, I took assertive action if someone stepped out of line. I remember one match the season after when we played Wigan away. We were losing 2-0 at half time and one player, who had been poor in training all week, came in and started chirping up, having a go. I stepped in and told him to think about his own performance before he criticised others. It was the right time. He was going through the motions and I don't think he had the self-awareness to realise that he was part of the problem.

That said, ironically I was less likely to pull up other players wearing the captain's armband under Darren Ferguson as manager than I had been when Paul Dickov was there and I had no official role. Under Paul I felt like it was my responsibility because I didn't think he felt comfortable telling them that they needed to do more.

Darren, though, had sat down with me and explained 'I want you to be captain but you don't need to go around telling people to do this, this and this, because I'll do that. If I see somebody slacking or not doing it I'll pull them aside.' The boundaries of my role depended on the situation and the environment.

At the age of 36, in the PFA League Two Team of the Year in 2017. Here with Eden Hazard.

© PA Images / Alamy Stock Photo

In summary, the desire to honour Grandad (Coppinger), the goals I set myself, my keenness to be a good captain and the motivation to ensure that Doncaster didn't become stuck in League Two created a huge burden and feeling of responsibility. That season was intense and when we secured promotion with several games to go the sense of release was overwhelming.

ANALYSIS

LEADERSHIP
AND COMMUNICATION

I accept teenage, aspiring footballers reading this book might be asking themselves why a chapter on leadership and communication is relevant to them. They might be thinking that all they need to do is prepare and play well. To some extent, I agree. That approach might work for them at that stage of their career, and I accept that leadership isn't for everyone. A cohesive team needs a mix of characters, including leaders and followers.

However, I don't think leadership is purely the responsibility of the people who have it on their job title at a football club or those who wear the captain's armband. You can never have too many leaders in a dressing room and there's no requirement to wait until you reach a certain age before you attempt to help and influence others. That doesn't mean that youngsters should pin older players to the dressing room walls and shout motivational advice in their faces! However, any footballer who develops skills in this area will find them to be an asset, both for their career and the team they play for.

DRIVE AND AMBITION

Before we get to the role of younger footballers, we need to acknowledge that leadership in professional football starts at the top. In this book I've already explained how chairman John Ryan's vision and passion was a driving force behind Doncaster's successes.

That also applies to the management and coaching staff. If you trace my career you'll find a direct link between my (and the team's) success on the field with managerial excellence. When I worked for the likes of Alan Irvine (Newcastle), Eamonn Dolan (Exeter) and Sean O'Driscoll (Doncaster) the team was well-drilled, worked hard and gelled together and that was reflected in the performances and results. No wonder the likes of Jürgen Klopp, Pep Guardiola and Jose Mourinho are paid the big bucks. They have proven over many years, all around the world, that they lead clubs to trophies.

DRESSING ROOM INFLUENCERS

Below the boardroom and the managerial and coaching staff then the requirement for leadership cascades down to the team's captain and the senior pros. There are lots of studies that highlight just how incredibly influential these people can be, acting as a bridge between the manager and the rest of the squad. They have a big say in the dressing room, set the tone and sometimes deal with issues before management is aware or needs to get involved.

Of course, that influence can work both ways. If, for instance, the senior pros don't rate the manager and become disengaged than that is probably going to lead to division and conflict. So it's essential to get them onside. Darren Ferguson told me that when he went to Preston he made a mistake in looking for confrontation and making enemies with senior pros. His dad (Sir Alex Ferguson) said to him that you don't have to look for confrontation, it will come and find you. I think he learned from making that mistake and worked with the older pros at Doncaster to help the team.

In an upcoming chapter on 'Professionalism' I've detailed some of the good pros who I admire and have become outstanding dressing room leaders. They are essential to success and when Leicester City shocked the football world and won the Premier League they had the likes of Wes Morgan, Robert Huth, Kasper Schmeichel and Jamie Vardy. At Liverpool there was Jordan Henderson, James Milner and Virgil Van Dijk. Some of them wore the armband, although I don't think that's essential to be seen as a 'leader'

▌DIFFERENT STYLES

There are different ways to lead but all of the players I've mentioned didn't just talk a good game, they led by example. In football – and most other workplaces – people pay much more attention to your actions than to your words. There's no point in motivational speeches if you don't back it up in your behaviour, both on and off the pitch.

As a captain, I almost led from the back. My personality is quieter and more reserved, reflective and analytical than most so I was more inclined to work one-to-one than talk to the whole dressing room and to listen rather than lecture.

That was my preferred style but I recognise that there are other ways and I think that Rob Jones and myself make an interesting comparison. We were both captains at Doncaster, both led the team to promotion and had similar values and standards – yet our styles couldn't have been more different. Rob led from the front. He was 6ft 6in, an absolute leader of men, in-your-face and up-and-at-'em; a fist-clencher who would bark orders at a group that would have gone to war for him. It felt like he would have carried us all on his

Listening. An underrated skill in football.

© HeatherKingPhotography

> 'Players that aren't true leaders but try to be, always bash other players after a mistake. True leaders on the pitch already assume others will make mistakes.'
>
> **Johann Cruyff**

back if needs be. I have total admiration for him and his approach undoubtedly worked. We had others at Doncaster – Neil Sullivan and Richie Wellens come to mind – who also set high standards, also had an edge and were vocal in demanding a lot from their teammates and kept them on their toes.

They were more in line with the traditional, direct approach in football and it worked that time. However, I also remember Richie Wellens said that later on he got to a stage where he was shouting, screaming and demanding more from players who couldn't do what he wanted them to do, and his words were hollow because he couldn't do it himself anymore either. Some players said, 'Who the **** does he think he is. I'm not listening to him.'

Leadership is a complex topic. There isn't one style that will always work, there isn't one 'right' way to be a leader that suits all situations and just because it worked well once doesn't mean it always will. A passionate, rousing team talk may be enough to gee up some players before a big game, but it may over-motivate others. If you're on the end of a big defeat, some players may react better to a hammering whilst others need an arm around their shoulder. Equally, if the feedback is always harsh and critical it runs the risk of not being listened to, yet praise and a softly-softly approach may not make any impact. It's possible to be too nice and too nurturing.

My view is that ideal is to be able to change your

approach. As I got older I realised that I needed to adapt to the situation, the level I was playing at, the players I was playing with and my surroundings. For instance, I couldn't demand the same standards from the players when we were in League Two as when we were in the Championship. I needed to be aware that they had different skill levels and ways of thinking.

Captaincy needed some sophisticated skills, understanding the group and building relationships with my teammates so that I learned how they reacted to certain styles and tones. That helped me judge when to take a firm approach and when words of encouragement were a better option. No doubt, in the heat of the moment, it's easy to misread the situation and get it wrong, not least because some of it is intuitive.

In short, I guess it's about balance and flexibility ...

▌ COMMUNICATION AND UNDERSTANDING OTHERS

... and communication skills. Whatever your approach you need to be able to communicate clearly and succinctly in a way that encourages people to listen, whether it's one-on-one or to the entire team. That's a solid foundation for all coaches, captains and leaders. Anyone can talk but not everyone develops the skills to motivate others, influence change and inspire others towards a set of goals.

Communication is a vital area in a team sport, particularly for its leaders. During my career I became better at adjusting my style to different teammates, managers and coaches in the way that I spoke to them,

With Ben Whiteman, a kindred spirit and an impressive young leader.

© HeatherKingPhotography

not just in the words I used but eye contact, gestures, facial expressions, tone of voice and so on.

YOUNG LEADERS

To go back to the start of the chapter, I just want to emphasise that there is no minimum age for leadership. It takes many forms. If you are inexperienced in the dressing room then your 'leadership' could involve just listening to a troubled teammate or showing some resilience when the going gets tough. It's possible to lead without saying a word. You can be a silent leader.

Ben Whiteman is a great example of a young man who has instincts to lead. He's ahead of his time in his maturity on and off the pitch, the way he goes about his business and the high standards that he sets, and demands of others, every day. When he became captain at Doncaster I became a confidant for him, speaking with him every day after training, before games, after games. We analysed performances and how the club was going. I loved his passion for the game.

Tom Anderson is the same. Leadership skills are a helpful attribute for a pro footballer and both of them have it in abundance. Despite their age, because they lead by example and because their actions match their words, they are respected and listened to by everyone in the dressing room.

TAKEAWAYS

- Leadership isn't just the responsibility of the people who have it on their job title or wear the captain's armband. There's no requirement to wait until you reach a certain age before you attempt to help and influence others.

- There are different styles of leadership and in football – and most other workplaces – people pay much more attention to your actions than to your words.

- Develop your communication skills, specifically body language and listening. It will help you in many situations.

EYEWITNESS

BEN WHITEMAN

It feels suitable that Ben Whiteman's contribution links the sections on leadership and professionalism. I've spent a lot of time with Ben and he is one of the most impressive young footballers and people whom I've worked with. He's dedicated to the game and was made captain at an unusually young age. I would say that he's an ideal role model for aspiring footballers if they want to make the most of their potential because of his professional mindset and leadership qualities. He left Doncaster at the start of 2021 to join Preston North End.

CAPTAINCY MATERIAL – 'I was captain of the local team at a very young age, made captain of Sheffield United under-23s and then progressed from there. In my second year at Doncaster I kicked on and became one of the key men and was given the captain's armband. If you're one of the key men it doesn't matter how old you are; as soon as you start talking, people start listening, although I do it constructively. I'm not just blasting players. Twenty years ago there were a lot of alpha-males in the dressing room, and you heard stories about training ground and dressing room bust-ups but I don't think that really happens anymore.

'I think my main strength as a captain is setting high standards – not just for me but everyone else. The main goal is to achieve things in football and if people aren't pulling their weight then you've got to clamp down on it. I'll be honest, and I don't beat around the bush. I've always been a very vocal person anyway.'

FLEXIBILITY – 'When somebody new comes into the building I'll stand back and watch what their character is like. Once you know someone on a personal basis then you can make a judgement. Everybody's different and a massive factor in leadership is that you can't just be the same with everybody. There's a time and a place both for an arm around the shoulder and giving someone a rocket. It's just how you manage different people. Communication is massive in delivering your message. If you can mix up your approach you're going to get the best outcome for the team – it's a team sport, it's not about individuals – and if you do that then you've got a great chance of succeeding.

'I'm a big Man United fan and I remember reading something on Sir Alex Ferguson where there were times when everyone else would get a rocket but Eric Cantona would get away with it. The Ferguson 'hair-dryer' treatment wouldn't work with him but he was often the match-winner at the weekend.'

POSITIVE INFLUENCE – 'My advice to young footballers is just be yourself. I know that sounds a cliché but some people don't really want to be vocal, and it comes more naturally to some than others. Not everyone is built to be a leader. In my opinion, the less dedicated players and the ones who don't love the game so much aren't really in a position to take on that role anyway because a leader should be someone who everyone looks up to in every aspect. But I believe that being seen as a captain and a positive influence on the dressing room by managers and coaches has definitely been an asset for my career so far.'

CONNECTION – 'One of the reasons why James and myself have got on so well is that we've got a lot in common. He had a similar route to me in the game: he left Newcastle when he was younger and I got released by Manchester United when I was 16 years old. It's very difficult to drag yourself up off the floor, particularly when it's your boyhood club, so we both showed grit and character to not give up and keep going.

'We also both just love football. I'm from a football-mad background, love watching it, love studying it, love coming into work each day. There's only a certain few who enjoy going out training, enjoy the preparation and building up to the game at the weekend, but James is also like that. If you don't love your job then you don't play until you're 40 years old!'

INFLUENCE – 'James has been the biggest influence on my career to date. When Darren Moore came in as manager at Doncaster I was made captain (Copps was made club captain) and had the armband but if there was one person you looked up to in the dressing room it was James Coppinger. Ask any lad around my age who's worked at Doncaster and they'll tell you that. He was head and shoulders above any footballer I've played with – both on and off the pitch.

'We spoke every day, mostly about football, but if I ever had a problem in my private life then I also spoke to James straight away. That hasn't changed now that I've left the club. He's my closest mate in football. '

MENTOR – 'James has definitely got the right skills and assets to be a great mentor. He's always honest, which I think is massive in football and life. He sees both sides. And a really skilled communicator. I've never really seen him get it wrong in the way he's delivered a message.'

PROFESSIONALISM

8

PROVING MY WORTH

AS A PROFESSIONAL footballer the psychological challenges kept on coming. As I entered the last few years of my career the fact that I had established a reputation within the club and the wider England Football League gave me no immunity from having to keep proving myself.

I've always felt uncomfortable being described as a legend but Donnie fans have taken me to their hearts, and I feel honoured and grateful.

© Doncaster Rovers Football Club

■ 'ONLY AS GOOD AS YOUR LAST GAME'

There's a saying in sport that you are only as good as your last game and I think that's true to some extent, particularly when you are in your late 30s. If you have one poor game supporters and the media start to whisper that you're over the hill. They couldn't pension me off because I'd already done that – collecting my Professional Footballers' Association (PFA) pension, as is the norm, at 35 – but I saw no reason to hang my boots up, not least because I'd grown to appreciate that my main motivation was to be happy, and I was happiest when I was playing football.

Besides, I still retained my technical and tactical skills, and, physically, didn't feel any different to when I was in my 20s. The sports scientists at the club told me that if anything my related data and statistics were improving. Recovery and recuperation after games wasn't an issue either. You hear stories of veteran footballers taking two or three days for their creaking limbs to recover from the exertions of each match. I felt none of that.

Yet when there's new management or coaching staff and they review their available resources there is always a danger that they don't fancy you as a player or see you as some kind of threat to their authority or position. And if you are on rolling one-year contracts – as I was at this stage – then you can quickly find yourself out of favour and isolated.

My approach to this challenge was to focus on what I could control and keep on doing what I was doing. I knew that every manager wants the best from the team and if I demonstrated a pro mindset every day then why wouldn't they want me to be a part of the set-up? I also adapted my communication to different characters, tried to understand what they wanted from me and give it to them. That didn't mean I was submissive – I challenged them as much as they challenged me – but I tried to work with them rather than against. Above all, I relished each new challenge. I didn't want to be part of the furniture and be given a contract based on reputation. My motivation every season was to prove my worth. Then, if I had done my part, it was up to the manager. I recognised I couldn't control them so there was no point worrying about that.

That exact scenario occurred at the start of the 2018/19 season. Having consolidated the team in League One the previous year with a 15th-place finish Darren Ferguson resigned as manager. He was replaced by the 38-year-old Northern Irishman Grant McCann and I was faced with the prospect of fighting to prove my worth to a new manager, less than a year older than me, who might prefer to move me on and focus on youth.

Although he chose to look elsewhere for his captain – opting to hand Tommy Rowe the armband – he gave me responsibility as overall club captain, trusted me and, best of all, played me. I repaid that faith with a personal best of 51 games, as we finished in sixth place, losing in the play-off semi-final to Charlton Athletic on penalties. That was enough to earn me another one-year contract in May 2019, although Grant then left to go to Hull and I was faced with yet another manager to build a relationship with and impress.

MENTOR

This time it was Darren Moore. Of course, my amount of game time reduced as my age increased and I found that frustrating because I felt no different physically, yet I could sympathise with the manager because I know he was juggling his resources and trying to keep everybody happy.

Besides I could also be valuable in my mentoring role. The departure of Tommy Rowe led to another switch in captaincy and Darren opted for a youthful appointment in Ben Whiteman, who I took under my wing.

It wasn't just Ben though. With age, experience and hundreds of games under my belt, I became seen – and saw myself – as a mentor. My teammates knew I was big on the mental side and that I had an open door for them to come and speak to me and ask me questions.

I remember a youngster who got subbed when he didn't think he should have been and didn't know what to do, and one who I spoke to after they were criticised by the manager. I was able to soften the blow, saying 'Don't take it to heart, he's only trying to do it for the team, you've been brilliant.'

PANDEMIC

Of course, everyone's mental health and resilience were tested in 2020 and 2021 when the coronavirus pandemic swept across the world. Our football season ended abruptly in March 2020 and suddenly sport seemed irrelevant. Aside from the effects of the virus, some players struggled to cope with the inactivity and uncertainty of the lockdown. They were unused to being home-bound and restricted and may have feared for their long-term futures because of the commercial consequences. I tried to help where I could.

This was another example of where my mentality helped me. Lucie, as a paediatric nurse, was on the front line and with three kids to look after my responsibilities and focus changed. I got on with it and made the best of the situation. I've learned over the years to adapt to what's happening around me; if I can't control it then I don't let it affect me.

▎SUPERMAN!

I didn't want to end my career in these circumstances and secured a contract extension to play during the 2020/21 season.

It was tough, though. We were restricted for much of the season to training in groups of three, four and five and were unable to shower, eat or congregate afterwards. Worse, there were no fans at the matches and my game time was limited. So there was still a danger of an anti-climactic end to my career.

Then, in February 2021 the season burst into life for me. My first game after turning 40 was against Hull City and to celebrate 17 years at Doncaster Rovers the club asked me and my two lads to design a special match-day kit. I loved the idea. Growing up I bought different kits from the market – I can instantly see the yellow of my Brazil kit and the orange of Holland – and felt like I turned into someone different when I put them on, like superman putting on his costume and cape!

The kit was in association with the mental health charity Campaign Against Living Miserably (CALM) and was mainly gold with a black and white sash, with personalised JC26 features. I've worn many different colours in my career but never gold which gave a retro, classy, commemorative feel. Certainly, it was popular, becoming the fastest-ever selling kit in the club's history. It soon sold out.

On the day of the match, the lads also presented me with some white-and-gold boots with my name on them. I'd just come back from an eight-week lay-off with a calf injury and started as a sub. So this spotlight on me felt a bit OTT and I felt a bit self-conscious when I was warming up, not helped by one of the Hull substitutes who asked, 'Are you the one who designed the crap kit? Aren't you a bit too old

In a kit I designed and wearing JC26 boots I was presented with, scoring a late equaliser against Hull City. A golden moment from my last season.

© HeatherKingPhotography

to be wearing those boots?' It was a bit of banter, which he maybe took a bit too far – but I was the one laughing at the end after I came on with five minutes of normal time left and scored an equaliser in the 12th minute of injury time with one of the best free-kicks of my career.

This was the law of attraction working again. I knew I was going to come on at the end, had visualised scoring a free-kick from exactly that position and so when the opportunity came up I had rehearsed it in my head, relished the pressure of the moment and expected to score.

A surreal, COVID-dominated last season.

© AHPIXPhotography

As I warmed down after the game on the pitch with the other subs I sought out the lad from Hull and gave him a bit of stick: 'I can get you one of these shirts and sign it for you if you want!' He didn't know how keen I've always been to prove people wrong.

■ 'EVERYTHING IS POSSIBLE, EVEN THE IMPOSSIBLE'

A week later, to mark my 800th appearance as a pro, I was put forward to receive the Honorary Freedom of Doncaster, one of the highest accolades I've received,

not least because I felt it was a reflection on me as a person as well as a footballer. I lived in Doncaster for ten years, my wife worked at the hospital there where my two boys were born and I think it's an unbelievable town where I've always been made welcome.

And then two days after that Darren Moore left Doncaster to take up the manager's role at Sheffield Wednesday, being replaced by Andy Butler, who I had worked with for many years. Under Andy I started more games, played well and, for a while, I warmed to the pleas of 'one more year!' from fans on social media.

9 May 2021. The end of the line. With my team mates before my 695th and final appearance for Doncaster Rovers.

© HeatherKingPhotography

Clarity and closure came when it was announced that I was the 2021 winner of the prestigious Tom Finney Award, an annual recognition presented to a player who is judged to have had an outstanding career and contributed an exceptional amount to the EFL and football in general. This was another massive honour and it made my mind up. A fitting way to end.

And so, on Sunday, 9 May 2021 I played my 817th (695th for Doncaster Rovers) and last game of professional football. Unfortunately, there wasn't a packed stadium but my family and friends were there and even during the game I distinctly heard the shouts and screams of encouragement from my seven-year-old daughter Phoebe. Phoebe is a different breed and afterwards she wanted to stay with me, soaking it all up and waiting with limitless patience as I held an emotional press conference and then spent more than an hour and a half outside the Keepmoat, signing autographs and thanking the hundreds of supporters who had gathered to say farewell. For her to witness that was magical and made it all worthwhile.

Normally at the end of a season I'm wiped out for two or three days, but this was different. Instead, I felt energised and excited by the future, not least the new role I had been offered within the club.

For 24 years I had devoted myself as a professional footballer; engrossed and focused, battling through the ups and downs, always pushing to maintain the standards of professionalism that I had set. Of course, I loved every minute but there was a price to pay. It took a lot out of me. Now, I could see more of my family and friends, go skiing for the first time and explore a range of exciting, new opportunities that I had been preparing for.

Since Phoebe was four years old every night before bed she has repeated back to me a saying that I shared with her: 'Everything is possible, even the impossible.' And those words never felt more relevant. This didn't feel much like an end, more a new beginning and an opportunity for me to use my skills in new areas.

ANALYSIS

PROFESSIONALISM

I mentioned at the end of the last section how the constant discipline and focus to maintain professional standards is critical to achieve long-term success but draining. It's so much more difficult if you don't feel it in your heart. So, the people in football I admire most and who have had the most impact on me are the good pros, the ones who live and breathe the game. I know they are motivated to do well for their families, for themselves and the teams they represent and, above all, for the love of the sport of football. Their passion is infectious and I love talking to them and being around them.

In my teenage days at Newcastle I was briefly in and around the likes of the sorely missed Gary Speed and Sir Bobby Robson. In some ways, it feels wrong to only pick out some characters from the hundreds I've worked with but I want to highlight three from my time at Doncaster Rovers who I particularly admired.

▌ROLE MODELS

Goalkeeper Neil Sullivan had played in the Premier League with Chelsea and Tottenham Hotspur and then with Leeds United in the Championship. He also played 28 times for Scotland. But he won his first trophy with Doncaster at the Millennium Stadium and you could see how much it meant to him. When he signed for us he was 36 and he played until he was 43 years old! He made the most of every single day; I can't remember one training session when he came in and went through the motions. Even in his 40s he'd be early in the gym, pounding the treadmill, trying to keep the weight off and keep his body keep ticking over.

Richie Wellens was at Manchester United, Blackpool and Oldham before I played with him at Doncaster when he got promoted to the Championship. We were a nicey-nicey team when he joined and he added the bite that we needed to be successful. If you weren't at it and you weren't playing well and didn't pass him the ball then he wouldn't stand for it. He would tell you in no uncertain terms. What a player though! I had an almost telepathic understanding with him on the pitch. We were on the same wavelength. Then he went to Leicester City and had a fantastic career there.

Billy Sharp was another with massive enthusiasm for football and, above all, scoring goals. I roomed with Billy and he was somebody who you could feed off. Billy was optimistic and ambitious, both for himself and the team, and thought everything was possible. That was true inside the penalty box. He didn't *hope* to score goals, he *expected* to. It was a pleasure for me, someone who enjoyed assisting goals as much as scoring them, to know he was going to be in the right place and that if I put the ball into certain areas of the pitch he would be there to tap them in. The number of goals he scored in the box was unreal, and he continues to do so. He has as much desire now to score goals as he did when he was 16 or 17. I've never met anybody apart from Alan Shearer who was so clinical in front of goal. Billy also has my complete admiration for the way that he has coped with personal challenges in his life outside of football.

What strikes me is that all three have heaps of personality and character; something about them; a spark and an energy that sets them apart.

▌LOYALTY

They are my examples from Doncaster but, perhaps for obvious reasons, I also have a particular affinity for the long-serving veterans who have shown loyalty to their club and a drive to maintain their dedication over years and years.

I'm thinking of Ryan Giggs at Manchester United and Steven Gerrard at Liverpool, who were sensational players over several decades. Currently, there's Dean Lewington at MK Dons, the current longest-serving player for a single club in the EFL, and Mark Noble at West Ham United, who's been there for more than 17 years. Then there are the super-elite European icons, such as Marcelo at Real Madrid and Giorgio Chiellini at Juventus, who have been first-teamers at two of the best clubs in the world for years and years.

Above all, there's the GOAT (Greatest Of All Time), Lionel Messi. He was at Barcelona for more than 20 years, from the age of 13 and made his first-team debut two months and two days after I first played for Doncaster Rovers. Messi, of course, has got it all: incredible technique, incredible awareness of the game around him, incredible pace and movement. But he couldn't have achieved so much for club and country without also being world-class in his professionalism and the grey matter that lies between his ears.

All of these players I've mentioned achieved their potential and earned their success because they developed a psychological performance that made them a fixture in their teams and helped them become a positive influence on the club, both on and off the pitch. Players have enjoyed a hot streak for a year or two but this group have played and contributed for 30 or 40 games, season after season. Managers and fans love them because of their enthusiasm, playing for the badge on the front of the shirt, rather than the name on the back.

I know there are people like this in most dressing rooms in professional sport. They're not at the level of a Messi and their achievements will vary based on technical skills, tactical awareness, physical attributes and intangibles such as luck, but in this chapter I want to write in some depth about professionalism and what it means in practical terms.

▌ATTRIBUTES

Firstly, it's fair to say that they are all the personification of all the attributes I've already written about in this book:

- Love of football
- Self-belief and confidence
- Self-awareness
- Accountability
- Consistency
- Teamwork
- Hard work
- Focus
- Communication skills
- Leadership
- Continuous improvement

All the footballers I've just referred to excel in these areas; however, professionalism has many forms and the day-to-day approach taken by each player will differ because each will have worked out a unique routine that gives them the best chance of playing well in each match.

▮PRACTICAL APPLICATION

Therefore what follows in this section doesn't come with a guarantee of success. It's not that easy I'm afraid! It's just *my* version of professionalism – in no particular order – that I've developed over the years. I've already shared most of those aspects in the book, so I'll mention most briefly here:

GOALS AND VISUALISATION – It's easy to focus on the achievements and forget that if the target had not been set and visualised then it may not have been possible. Moments like my hat-trick against Southend in the play-offs and my free-kick against Hull for Doncaster weren't lucky. They were part of a process.

NUTRITION AND HYDRATION – I believed in moderation. No specific diets, no magic formula, nothing weird or wonderful. As I matured the drinking of alcohol reduced. At Exeter it was twice a week on average; when I went to Doncaster it was once a week; by the age of 30 it was once a month; at 35 it was once every three months and in the past two years it's been once every six months.

DECISION-MAKING – When I made big strategic decisions about my career – such as whether to move clubs – I was always influenced by loyalty, personal fulfilment and enjoyment rather than chasing money or status. I followed that philosophy when I chose to leave a Premier League club and when I stayed loyal to Doncaster Rovers despite being wanted by several clubs who offered more money.

Out with the lads. I adopted a more professional mindset as my career developed, and these outings became less frequent and less boozy!
© James Coppinger

FOCUS AND DISCIPLINE – I increasingly trained and played at 100 per cent commitment and focus every day. I ate and slept football, 24/7. I sacrificed a lot, including missing out on many social events such as birthday parties and Christmas socialising that I would have enjoyed, and for 20 years I wasn't able to fully switch off during the season. That lifestyle could be seen as dull but professional sport can be more about dedication than flair, more about perspiration than inspiration. No wonder that when we got to each summer break I was done for two or three days because that constant need for focus and discipline had quite an effect on my body and mental state.

RUNNING AND STRETCHING – My version of professionalism involved more running and soft-tissue stretching than weights. I've been encouraged to bulk up but, having weighed up the pros and cons, decided against it because my approach allowed me to consistently play three 90-minute games a week, covering anything up to 12 kilometres per game, free from injuries. Even at 40 years old I felt supple and hardly ever felt stiffness after a game.

MATCH-DAY PREPARATION – My routine was standard. I wasn't like some teammates who followed superstitions. My confidence came because I developed total trust in my ability to perform on a match-day, letting my muscle memory and experience take care of my performance. I didn't waste energy worrying about what might happen and getting nervous. I turned up at the stadium fresh and keen to play.

ANALYSIS – I watched re-runs of my matches since I was primary school age when my grandads used to video the games. I always enjoyed replaying when it had gone well – and if it had gone badly then a lot of times I found it wasn't as bad as I thought when I watched it back. It was sometimes difficult to watch if I had a shocker but it was the best way of learning and helped me work out what went wrong.

Towards the end of my career, like the other players, I got sent clips of my contributions within a game on an app – and sometimes the manager would pick out certain incidents from a game at a team meeting. By then there was also a lot of data available. I looked at my running stats but not the intensity of the runs. It was just working out what felt relevant and was helpful.

CURIOSITY AND WANTING TO LEARN – That analysis and receptiveness to feedback became an essential part of my improvement. I became more humble and open to trying to new things to help me become not just a better footballer but a better husband, father and friend.

SOCIAL GROUPS – Over the years I became more assertive and choosy about how and where I spent my time and with whom. Most of the time I was with my family and a small group of people who I deeply care about and care about me. I avoided negative or unhelpful influences.

■ WAYS OF WORKING

That was the way I went about my business but bear in mind that the progression was developed over 20 years in the game, continued to evolve right through to the end of my career and might not necessarily work for others. Even then I kept making tweaks and there were days where my approach didn't provide me with the results I wanted. However, I had total confidence that, in general, this was what worked best for me and I was single-minded in following it. In my last year a coach described me as selfish in a good way; a team-player but someone who knew what he wanted and went and got it.

My suggestion to aspiring footballers is to assess themselves against the shared traits of professionalism that I outlined earlier in the chapter – such as self-belief and resilience. Then develop strategies to improve, and implement a consistent and practical way of working that gives them the best chance to be successful.

A good example of that is physical conditioning and gym work. Find a programme that specifically works for you and the position you play. If you're a centre half you might need to get stronger; if you're a winger you might want to get quicker. Work with the sports science staff, the coaches and the manager. Appreciate you are an athlete as well as a footballer.

Finally, understand that a professional mindset takes time. Footballers develop their abilities over years of consistent training and competition. It's a step-by-step progression. Don't seek instant gratification and easy fixes. Recognise that this is a long, slow journey with many bumps on the road, and if you are aware of this, prepared to dedicate yourself and work hard, then you will stand out. That's the key to help you maximise your potential.

TAKEAWAYS

■ Professionalism takes many forms and your day-to-day routine should be tailored to give you the best chance of consistent success.

■ The best pros live and breathe the game and ooze personality and character. They are motivated to do well for their families, for themselves, for the teams they represent and, above all, for the love of the sport of football.

■ A pro mindset takes years of training and competition to develop. It's a long, slow journey with many bumps on the road, and if you are aware of this, prepared to dedicate yourself and work hard, then you will stand out.

PEOPLE FIRST, FOOTBALLERS SECOND 9

I BELIEVE THAT for aspiring professional footballers the most critical time is around the age of 16 years old. That's when the elites who have excelled in Academies get offered a two-year scholarship with a club. Once they get beyond the excitement of having been chosen the reality sets they are still a long way from having made it. Yes, the opportunity exists but it starts with leaving the education system and entering an adult workplace for the first time – and when that workplace is the professional football industry then it's a double dose of reality and, for many, a massive shock. It's make or break, sink or swim. They've got just 16 to 18 months to prove themselves and justify receiving a professional contract. Suddenly they are training every day, assessed every day and constantly under pressure to impress.

So I strongly feel that during the scholarship youngsters at every club need constant support and guidance. They need somebody who is there on a fortnightly or monthly basis to help them through the process. The ones who earn a contract, in my experience, will have tactical, technical and physical abilities and, most importantly, mental strength.

That's the case at youth level and increasingly across all recruitment. For instance, Graham Potter, a highly rated young manager, ensures that all levels of recruitment at the club take into account mentality rather than just footballing experience: 'Experience isn't necessarily positive,' he has said. 'It depends on what type of experience it is and what they bring and what the mentality is. For me it is more about the individual, the personality, what they believe they can do, how coachable and how much they want to be part of what we are trying to achieve.'

■ 'MENTAL TRAINING IS THE FUTURE FOR FOOTBALL'

People have attached a stigma to psychological performance in sport but, slowly, football is waking up to its importance and it will take off over the next five to ten years. With social media, with the expectancy of performance, with the money, with all the things that are coming into the professional game, there's going to be a need to support the players.

The most forward-thinking clubs and managers in the modern game already *get* the importance and have it at the forefront of everything they do.

The England manager, Gareth Southgate, has experienced the ups and downs of elite sport and knows the full range of psychological challenges that a footballer experiences. He once said that 'the defining factor in a successful professional is mentality' and that belief has been clear in his mature and empathetic leadership of the national team. He *gets* it.

The approaches of other world-class coaches in the modern era, such as Jürgen Klopp, Pep Guardiola and Jose Mourinho, are also light years away from the traditional, autonomous style of management that was previously popular in England. They may employ specialists such as sports psychologists and/or the management team may adopt a leadership style that recognises its importance.

Brendan Rodgers is another who *gets* it. He has said, 'I think psychology is massive. I have found that part of the game fascinating, in terms of getting the best out of people ... I think a lot of work goes into the technical, the tactical and obviously the physical, but the mental aspect is about managing the pressure and the stress and being consistent. That is obviously the key. I tend to focus on that quite a lot.'

▌'PEOPLE AND SOCIETY HAVE CHANGED'

That 'focus' doesn't mean these managers are cuddly and soft and can be taken advantage of. Far from it; they have all proved they are serial winners and incredibly competitive. However, they recognise they're managing people first, footballers second. In their different styles they are all brilliant communicators and I genuinely think that to be a coach or manager you now need to be able to speak with your players in a more sophisticated and empathic way than before. People and society have changed.

I hope that this book has helped to de-stigmatise the subject of mindset and shown that to develop skills in this area does not involve filling the players' heads with academic theories and mumbo-jumbo. It starts with education on how the brain works and how it all joins up: our thoughts dictate how we feel, how we feel dictates how we act, and how we act determines our results.

That's quite a bombshell for some. Then it's as simple as being honest with yourself, understanding where you are, understanding where you want to be and then thinking 'right, how am I going to change my thinking to get there?' With support and guidance, a plan gets created and can be put into practice, day by day.

As I've hopefully demonstrated there are so many areas where mental skills can help. Certainly, I've watched players with unbelievable potential and ability struggle with injuries, loss of form, expectations, and personal issues because they didn't know how to get their heads around the challenges they face.

UNLOCKING POTENTIAL

Post-playing, part of my role will be to offer support and guidance to aspiring footballers, sharing my experience, helping them to acquire tools and techniques to unlock their potential. Having played the game for so long I've probably been in their position, made mistakes and improved my approach. I can speak their language and the feedback I've had suggests that I'm real and authentic and can communicate in a way that brings the theory to life in a football context.

Of course, it's an advantage if you know how players react to certain circumstances. I've been in so many

With my two boys. Both love their football but if they do want to consider it as a career the odds will inevitably be stacked against them in an incredibly competitive industry. Mindset will be key!
© Doncaster Rovers Football Club

meetings where we've had somebody come in to try and work with the team or promote something and they've fallen flat on their face because they've gone about it the wrong way. The majority of footballers learn by doing and seeing, not by writing or sitting in a room for 45 minutes, listening to somebody talk and thinking 'the last thing I want to be doing is sat here'. They need to be active to switch on.

I've also learnt in the work that I've done so far that when working one to one, the communication and mentoring needs to be tailored to each individual. I start by sitting down, talking and asking questions. Every single set of answers will be different because every player has been conditioned differently. They function differently, behave differently and have created a unique mind-map. So I need to adapt and adjust my approach to them and their learning style. Ultimately, though, for the relationship to work well we need the same traits that I highlighted under Sean O'Driscoll's successful Doncaster team: trust, respect and honesty.

I know that kind of dialogue will occasionally bring to the surface issues and challenges that go beyond sport. That is so important. Some people bottle things up and are concerned they may appear weak if they talk about them. It's quite the reverse and when people open their hearts and bare their souls then the benefits for their mental health, as well as sporting performance, can be significant. I've found that it is important to give them space and use silence constructively rather than feel uncomfortable with it and fill the gaps.

Even at the upper echelons of the game, being able to talk can be a release. The England international full-back, Ben Chilwell, wrote on social media about a time at Leicester City: 'Last year I went through a period where my confidence took a hit and it affected me in my everyday life. I eventually spoke to someone about it and I found it helped a lot. In football especially, people don't like to show weakness. But talking about difficulties or problems in your life with others is important.'

I've already had conversations with mentees who have said, 'You'll never know how much speaking to you has changed my life.' That makes it all worthwhile.

Particularly in my last season, I mentored players at a range of different clubs. I felt immense satisfaction that an 18-year-old who I had mentored through a difficult season made his league debut on the same day that I played my last. That felt right; a sense of the wheel turning; one career finishing as another started.

Part of my new, non-playing role at Doncaster focuses on mental performance, providing mentorship, advice, and guidance to staff and players from the academy up to the first team. What an exciting opportunity: using my knowledge and experience to give something back and help others to fulfil their potential. If you've reached this far into the book it will come as no surprise that I will be promoting the fact that the way we think affects the results we achieve, and we can all change the way we think. Football, like life, is played as much in the head as on the pitch.

CAREER STATISTICS

CLUB	SEASON	DIVISION	STARTS	SUB.	GOALS
Newcastle United	1999/2000	Premier League	0	0	0
	2000/01	Premier League	0	1	0
	2001/02	Premier League	0	0	0
		TOTAL	0 (0%)	1 (100%)	0
Hartlepool United	1999/2000	Third Division	8	4	3
	2001/02	Third Division	14	0	2
		Total	22 (85%)	4 (15%)	5
Exeter City	2002/03	Third Division	41	8	5
	2003/04	Football Conference	37	3	9
		TOTAL	78 (88%)	11 (12%)	14

Doncaster Rovers	2004/05	League One	31	7	0
	2005/06	League One	38	5	5
	2006/07	League One	39	9	5
	2007/08	League One	37	9	6
	2008/09	Championship	33	4	5
	2009/10	Championship	41	1	5
	2010/11	Championship	40	2	7
	2011/12	Championship	33	7	2
	2012/13	League One	21	6	2
	2013/14	Championship	36	7	4
	2014/15	League One	41	2	6
	2015/16	League One	43	1	3
	2016/17	League Two	38	1	10
	2017/18	League One	37	5	5

Doncaster Rovers	2018/19	League One	45	6	4
	2019/20	League One	28	5	4
	2020/21	League One	22	15	5
	TOTAL		**603 [87%]**	**92 [13%]**	**78**
Nottingham Forest	2012/13	Championship	2	4	0
	TOTAL		2	4	0
OVERALL CAREER TOTAL			**705 [86%]**	**112 [14%]**	**97**

■ DONCASTER ROVERS – LEADING APPEARANCE MAKER

James Coppinger – 695 games

Colin Douglas – 468 games

Fred Emery – 438 games

Bert Tindill – 429 games

Brian Makepeace – 378 games

EYEWITNESS

ANDREW TAYLOR

It felt right to finish the book with the last 'Eyewitness' account, and an adapted version of a kind article that was written for **Doncaster Free Press** *during my last season as a professional. During my time at the club lifelong supporter Andrew Taylor has watched more games than most, home and away. So few are in a better position to analyse my contribution to the club.*

I think most people would describe me as a humble and modest guy but, at the risk of being self-indulgent, I wanted to include the article because it reflects precisely how I would want to be remembered by the Doncaster fans. If Andrew has managed to capture a sense of how I am judged then that makes me feel very grateful and proud.

Slowly but surely, I am coming to terms with the idea that over the last 17 seasons I've become so accustomed to seeing Coppinger's name on the Rovers teamsheet that my mind now considers it a certainty of life when in fact it never was.

Like many a helpless defender, I was sure Coppinger was always going to be there only to find that he isn't.

Liverpool fans, what did you do when Gerrard called it a day? Ultras of Roma, how did you adapt when Totti retired? Is there a sort of group therapy we can attend, surely there's at least a pamphlet?

Knowing that pamphlets for such things were a fantasy, I took some time to think back to Coppinger's and the Rovers' love affair.

Coppinger's arrival at Doncaster Rovers barely registered with me. What I didn't know at the time was that Rovers had just picked up the Wonka Bar with the golden ticket.

But it wasn't love at first sight.

It seemed to take Coppinger a couple of seasons to win the Rovers faithful over.

Coppinger offered glimpses of what was to come but not consistently. A moment of magic followed by an apparent lack of concentration.

Patience was a requirement for the love to blossom. It was worth it.

Before Coppinger (BC) I'd spent my entire youth with my neck craned in the air as Rovers players paid no regard to gravity or the turf they were playing on, playing a sort of 'hoof it tennis' with the opposition back four.

With Coppinger at Doncaster (AD) I was now witnessing something completely alien.

Coppinger, with the help of Jamie Paterson and Michael McIndoe, was suddenly paying as much attention to gravity as Isaac Newton.

Coppinger was now caressing passes to teammates, treating the Belle Vue turf like his grandmother's carpet and putting chiropractors in the Doncaster area out of pocket.

Under Sean O'Driscoll, the Rovers and Coppinger evolved to provide one of the greatest eras in our recent history. O'Driscoll seemed to earmark Coppinger as the blueprint of his sharp, fluid philosophy and brought in players that complemented him perfectly.

Thinking back to the O'Driscoll era it was as though Coppinger, Richie Wellens and Brian Stock were communicating on a different wavelength to everybody else, tessellating the ball to one another in tight triangles, playing football as though they were raised together from birth.

Pre-game, the referees gave regular instructions to 19 of the 22 players. To Coppinger, Wellens and Stock it was two touches maximum, a third and you'll be in the book son.

Throughout the O'Driscoll era there was a confidence I have not experienced before or afterwards watching the Rovers.

A confidence exerted to me and presumably others in the Keepmoat crowd, confidence that we will win today and that even if we don't, we will certainly have played the better football.

The eras, the appearances, goals and records can all be measured.

But what about the intangibles?

© AHPiXPhotography

The things we can't measure, the feelings that Coppinger exudes to the Rovers crowd each time he puts on the red and white, the individual memories Coppinger has given to each Rovers fan.

Those small, and sometimes insignificant to the result, moments of awe that make you look at the stranger next to you and make the universal facial expression of 'did you just see that?!'

The Southend hat-trick.

The Brentford winner.

Amongst my favourites stand out two moments.

Coppinger scored the leveller against Rotherham in the last South Yorkshire derby at the Keepmoat in 2019.

Although the goal wasn't Coppinger's cleanest connection with the ball, you couldn't find a single Donny fan that didn't feel connected to one another as the stadium erupted, but it was Coppinger's celebration that stuck with me.

Fate hasn't allowed Rovers and Rotherham to cross paths too many times in Coppinger's career.

As the ball bobbled over the line in front of the South Stand you could almost feel that Coppinger knew a derby leveller was one of the few milestones he was yet to reach in a Rovers shirt.

Adrenaline flowing and arms spread wide, Coppinger began to race over to the away end to celebrate and duly become the bullseye of every Rotherham fans' dartboard. However, the south goal to the away end is a fair distance and before Coppinger had even reached the halfway line he came to an abrupt stop. I like to think that as Coppinger's adrenaline wore off, his class kicked in and he thought twice about rubbing the Rotherham fans' noses in it.

Passion accompanied with dignity. A small embodiment of Coppinger's long Rovers career.

My second most cherished memory came against Burton last season.

Rovers goalkeeper Seny Dieng rushed out from his goal to clear a loose ball and prevent a Burton attack.

Dieng thumped the ball clear but caught it too cleanly and the ball was travelling fast, low and seemingly forever parallel to the earth's surface at knee height, on course for either Coppinger or a Burton attacker to pounce upon in the Doncaster half.

Dieng far from his goal, there was an obvious sense of panic in the air at the Keepmoat.

Coppinger, with a Burton attacker breathing down his neck and a ball soaring towards him like a bullet, managed in one David Blaine-esque touch to stop the bullet mid-flight as he controlled the ball and clipped it over the Burton attacker.

The ball, confused as to why all the g-force has suddenly dissipated, arched over the Burton player through the air and, as Coppinger pirouetted 180 degrees on one of the many sixpences he presumably spreads across the Keepmoat turf before each game, landed gracefully on his toe.

Coppinger then calmly strode forward and played a trademark measured through ball as butterflies appeared and birdsong was heard in what now appeared to be a different universe to the panicked Keepmoat of a few seconds before.

Once I'd picked my jaw out of my Bovril, I was left thinking what an injustice it is that these moments of awe that Coppinger regularly leaves behind to us lucky few are not filmed at every angle, compilated and posted on YouTube for us all to watch and re-watch.

For my money, if that particular moment was captured, it would rival any clip of the world's biggest stars.

Beyond the eras he has helped define and beyond the memories, there also lies what Coppinger has come to represent for Doncaster Rovers. Our identity.

Being a Rovers fan, we've always felt a bit different to the others.

Our identity has always seemed unique. We were the laughing stock of the country. Then we were the pub team having a laugh. We became the Arsenal of the North.

For the last decade, I have identified the Rovers with being the club that defies modern football, the club that evokes old fashioned values of heritage and loyalty. Coppinger's club.

In his final season Coppinger's involvement at the Keepmoat on a Saturday afternoon became less certain.

But what was certain is his place in our history, the identity he helped form, the many memories that are destined to become folklore, to be passed down by Rovers old timers in rocking chairs to kids and grandkids.

'Did you just see that?' Yes, we are the lucky ones that did.